CW00418409

BERLIN
TRAVEL GUIDE
2024

THE ULTIMATE TRAVEL GUIDE OF BERLIN

AUSTIN F. HUGHES

BERLIN TRAVEL GUIDE 2024
The Ultimate Travel Guide of Berlin.

© Austin F. Hughes
© E.G.P. Editorial

Printed in USA.
ISBN-13: 9798390160442

Copyright ©
All rights reserved.

BERLIN
TRAVEL GUIDE 2024

THE MOST POPULAR PLACES IN BERLIN

Berlin, the thriving capital of Germany, is a city of contrasts and contradictions. From its tumultuous history to its innovative spirit, Berlin is a melting pot of cultures and experiences.

The city boasts a wealth of attractions, from world-renowned museums and theaters to vibrant shopping districts and galleries. Take a stroll down the picturesque walks, sample the delectable cuisine at charming restaurants, and experience the thriving nightlife.

Berlin is also a haven for families, with a plethora of kid-friendly activities and sights. This guidebook, "List of the 100 most popular places in Berlin," is an all-encompassing guide that explores the city's top destinations.

From attractions and shops to tours and walks, this comprehensive guide covers it all.

Happy travels!

TABLE OF CONTENTS

ATTRACTIONS

BRANDENBURG GATE

Address: Pariser Platz, 10117 Berlin, Germany.

Historical background: The Brandenburg Gate is a symbol of the divided Germany and a symbol of unity since the fall of the Berlin Wall. It was built in the late 18th century and has undergone many changes throughout its history, including serving as a backdrop for speeches by Nazi leaders and as the site of a peaceful protest in 1989 that led to the fall of the Berlin Wall.

Practical information: The Brandenburg Gate is open 24 hours a day and admission is free. Visitors can walk through the gate and enjoy the surrounding park and nearby attractions, such as the Reichstag Building and the Berlin Wall Memorial.

Highlights and must-sees: Visitors can take in the grandeur of the Brandenburg Gate, which is one of the most recognizable landmarks in Berlin. The surrounding park is also a great place to relax and people-watch.

Cost: Admission to the Brandenburg Gate is free.

Quality: The Brandenburg Gate is well-maintained and offers a unique historical and cultural experience for visitors.

Curiosity and facts: The Brandenburg Gate wasmodeled after the Acropolis in Athens and was once part of the city wall that surrounded Berlin.

Advice: Visitors should be prepared to walk and spend time outside, as there is limited seating available.

Getting there: The Brandenburg Gate is located in the heart of Berlin and is easily accessible by public transportation, including the U-Bahn and S-Bahn.

Nearby attractions: The Reichstag Building, Berlin Wall Memorial, Berlin Zoo, and Pergamon Museum are all within walking distance of the Brandenburg Gate.

REICHSTAG BUILDING

Address: Platz der Republik 1, 11011 Berlin, Germany.

Historical background: The Reichstag Building was the home of the German parliament from 1894 to 1933. It was severely damaged in a fire in 1933 and lay in ruins until its reconstruction in the 1990s.

Practical information: The Reichstag Building is open daily and admission is free. Visitors can take a guided tour or climb to the top of the building for panoramic views of Berlin.

Highlights and must-sees: Visitors can explore the history of the Reichstag Building and learn about its role in the formation of the German government. The building's dome is a must-see for its panoramic views of Berlin.

Cost: Admission to the Reichstag Building is free, but visitors are required to book a time slot in advance to ensure security.

Quality: The Reichstag Building is a modern, well-maintained building that offers a unique historical and cultural experience for visitors.

Curiosity and facts: The Reichstag Building was reconstructed using environmentally friendly methods and features a glass dome that allows natural light to enter the building.

Advice: Visitors should book their time slot in advance to ensure entry and be prepared for security checks before entering the building.

Getting there: The Reichstag Building is located in the heart of Berlin and is easily accessible by public transportation, including the U-Bahn and S-Bahn.

Nearby attractions: The Brandenburg Gate, Berlin Wall Memorial, Berlin Zoo, and Pergamon Museum are all within walking distance of the Reichstag Building.

BERLIN WALL MEMORIAL

Address: Bernauer Str. 111, 13355 Berlin, Germany.

Historical background: The Berlin Wall Memorial is a memorial to the victims of the Berlin Wall and a reminder of the division of Germany. It is located on the site where the Berlin Wall once stood and includes a section of the original wall, a visitorscenter, and exhibitions about the history of the wall.

Practical information: The Berlin Wall Memorial is open daily and admission is free. Visitors can take a guided tour or explore the exhibitions and memorial on their own.

Highlights and must-sees: Visitors can see a section of the original Berlin Wall and learn about its history and the impact it had on the people of Berlin and Germany as a whole.

Cost: Admission to the Berlin Wall Memorial is free.

Quality: The Berlin Wall Memorial is well-maintained and offers a unique historical and cultural experience for visitors.

Curiosity and facts: The Berlin Wall was a physical symbol of the division between East and West Germany and stood from 1961 to 1989.

Advice: Visitors should be prepared to walk and spend time outside, as there is limited seating available.

Getting there: The Berlin Wall Memorial is located in the heart of Berlin and is easily accessible by public transportation, including the U-Bahn and S-Bahn.

Nearby attractions: The Brandenburg Gate, Reichstag Building, Berlin Zoo, and Pergamon Museum are all within walking distance of the Berlin Wall Memorial.

BERLIN ZOO

Address: Hardenbergplatz 8, 10787 Berlin, Germany.

Historical background: The Berlin Zoo is one of the oldest zoos in the world, having opened its doors in 1844. It is home to over 20,000 animals from all over the world and is a popular attraction for visitors of all ages.

Practical information: The Berlin Zoo is open daily and admission is charged. Visitors can purchase tickets in advance or at the entrance and can spend the day exploring the zoo and its many exhibits and attractions.

Highlights and must-sees: Visitors can see a wide range of animals, including elephants, lions, monkeys, and penguins, and enjoy interactive exhibits, such as the animal petting zoo and the aquarium.

Cost: Admission to the Berlin Zoo is charged and prices vary depending on the time of year and type of ticket purchased.

Quality: The Berlin Zoo is well-maintained and offers a fun and educational experience for visitors of all ages.

Curiosity and facts: The Berlin Zoo is one of the most visited zoos in the world and is home to over 20,000 animals from all over the world.

Advice: Visitors should be prepared to spend several hours at the zoo and wear comfortable walking shoes.

Getting there: The Berlin Zoo is located in the heart of Berlin and is easily accessible by public transportation, including the U-Bahn and S-Bahn.

Nearby attractions: The Brandenburg Gate, Reichstag Building, Berlin Wall Memorial, and Pergamon Museum are all within walking distance of the Berlin Zoo.

PERGAMON MUSEUM

Address: Am Kupfergraben 5, 10117 Berlin, Germany.

Historical background: The Pergamon Museum is one of the largest museums in Berlin and is home to a vast collection of ancient artifacts from the Middle East and Greece. It was opened in 1930 and has been a popular attraction for visitors of all ages for nearly a century.

Practical information: The Pergamon Museum is open daily and admission is charged. Visitors can purchase tickets in advance or at the entrance and can spend the day exploring the museum and its many exhibits and attractions.

Highlights and must-sees: Visitors can see the famous Pergamon Altar, the Ishtar Gate of Babylon, and the Market Gate of Miletus, among other ancient artifacts and structures.

Cost: Admission to the Pergamon Museum is charged and prices vary depending on the time of year and type of ticket purchased.

Quality: The Pergamon Museum is well-maintained and offers a unique and educational experience for visitors interested in ancient history and archaeology.

Curiosity and facts: The Pergamon Museum is home to some of the most famous ancient artifacts in the world, including the Pergamon Altar and the Ishtar Gate of Babylon.

Advice: Visitors should be prepared to spend several hours at the museum and wear comfortable walking shoes.

Getting there: The Pergamon Museum is located in the heart of Berlin and is easily accessible by public transportation, including the U-Bahn and S-Bahn.

Nearby attractions: The Brandenburg Gate, Reichstag Building, Berlin Wall Memorial, and Berlin Zoo are all within walking distance of the Pergamon Museum.

MUSEUM ISLAND

Address: Museum Island, 10178 Berlin, Germany.

Historical background: Museum Island is a group of five museums located on an island in the River Spree in Berlin. It is home to some of the most important collections of art and artifacts in the world, including the Alte Nationalgalerie, the Alte Museum, the Bode Museum, the Neues Museum, and the Pergamon Museum.

Practical information: Museum Island is open daily and admission is charged for each museum. Visitors can purchase tickets for individual museums or a combination ticket for all five museums. Each museum has its own hours of operation and visitors are advised to check in advance.

Highlights and must-sees: Visitors can explore the collections of art and artifacts at each of the five museums on Museum Island, including ancient sculptures, paintings, and other treasures from around the world.

Cost: Admission to each museum on Museum Island is charged and prices vary depending on the museum and type of ticket purchased.

Quality: Museum Island is home to some of the most important collections of art and artifacts in the world and is well-maintained and well-preserved for visitors to enjoy.

Curiosity and facts: Museum Island was designated a UNESCO World Heritage Site in 1999 and is home to some of the most famous museums in the world.

Advice: Visitors should plan their visit in advance and be prepared to spend several hours at each museum. Comfortable walking shoes are recommended.

Getting there: Museum Island is located in the heart of Berlin and is easily accessible by public transportation, including the U-Bahn and S-Bahn.

Nearby attractions: The Brandenburg Gate, Reichstag Building, Berlin Wall Memorial, Berlin Zoo, and Pergamon Museum are all within walking distance of Museum Island.

BERLIN CATHEDRAL

Address: Am Lustgarten, 10178 Berlin, Germany.

Historical background: The Berlin Cathedral is a Protestant church located in the heart of Berlin. It was built in the late 19th and early 20th centuries and is one of the largest and most recognizable churches in Germany.

Practical information: The Berlin Cathedral is open daily and admission is free. Visitors can tour the cathedral and enjoy the surrounding park and nearby attractions, such as the Reichstag Building and the Berlin Wall Memorial.

Highlights and must sees: Visitors can admire the grand interior of the Berlin Cathedral, including its ornate stained glass windows and grand organ, and enjoy views of the city from the cathedral's tower.

Cost: Admission to the Berlin Cathedral is free.

Quality: The Berlin Cathedral is well-maintained and offers a unique religious and cultural experience for visitors.

Curiosity and facts: The Berlin Cathedral is one of the largest churches in Germany and is recognized for its distinctive green dome and ornate interior.

Advice: Visitors should be prepared to climb stairs to reach the top of the cathedral's tower, and dress appropriately for visiting a religious site.

Getting there: The Berlin Cathedral is located in the heart of Berlin and is easily accessible by public transportation, including the U-Bahn and S-Bahn.

Nearby attractions: The Brandenburg Gate, Reichstag Building, Berlin Wall Memorial, Berlin Zoo, Pergamon Museum, and Museum Island are all within walking distance of the Berlin Cathedral.

ALEXANDERPLATZ

Address: Alexanderplatz, 10178 Berlin, Germany.

Historical background: Alexanderplatz is a large public square located in the heart of Berlin. It has been a central hub for transportation and commerce for centuries and is now a popular tourist destination, offering a variety of shopping, dining, and entertainment options.

Practical information: Alexanderplatz is open 24/7 and admission is free. Visitors can explore the square and its many shops, restaurants, and attractions at any time.

Highlights and must-sees: Visitors can enjoy the vibrant atmosphere of Alexanderplatz, visit the nearby Berlin TV

Tower, or explore the nearby Berlin Zoo and Pergamon Museum.

Cost: Admission to Alexanderplatz is free, but visitors may need to pay for individual attractions or activities within the square.

Quality: Alexanderplatz is well-maintained and offers a bustling, lively atmosphere for visitors to enjoy.

Curiosity and facts: Alexanderplatzis one of the largest public squares in Europe and is a popular destination for tourists and locals alike.

Advice: Visitors should be prepared for large crowds, especially on weekends and during peak tourist season.

Getting there: Alexanderplatz is located in the heart of Berlin and is easily accessible by public transportation, including the U-Bahn and S-Bahn.

Nearby attractions: The Brandenburg Gate, Reichstag Building, Berlin Wall Memorial, Berlin Zoo, Pergamon Museum, Museum Island, and Berlin Cathedral are all within walking distance of Alexanderplatz.

POTSDAMER PLATZ

Address: Potsdamer Platz, 10785 Berlin, Germany.

Historical background: Potsdamer Platz is a bustling public square located in the heart of Berlin. It was once one of the busiest intersections in Europe, but was destroyed during World War II. Today, it has been rebuilt as a modern commercial and entertainment hub, offering a variety of shopping, dining, and entertainment options.

Practical information: Potsdamer Platz is open 24/7 and admission is free. Visitors can explore the square and its many shops, restaurants, and attractions at any time.

Highlights and must-sees: Visitors can enjoy the modern atmosphere of Potsdamer Platz, visit the nearby Berlin Film Museum, or explore the nearby Berlin Zoo and Pergamon Museum.

Cost: Admission to Potsdamer Platz is free, but visitors may need to pay for individual attractions or activities within the square.

Quality: Potsdamer Platz is well-maintained and offers a vibrant, modern atmosphere for visitors to enjoy.

Curiosity and facts: Potsdamer Platz was one of the busiest intersections in Europe before World War II and has since been rebuilt as a modern commercial and entertainment hub.

Advice: Visitors should be prepared for large crowds, especially on weekends and during peak tourist season.

Getting there: Potsdamer Platz is located in the heart of Berlin and is easily accessible by public transportation, including the U-Bahn and S-Bahn.

Nearby attractions: The Brandenburg Gate, Reichstag Building, Berlin Wall Memorial, Berlin Zoo, Pergamon Museum, Museum Island, Berlin Cathedral, and Alexanderplatz are all within walking distance of Potsdamer Platz.

BERLIN TV TOWER

Address: Panoramastr. 1A, 10178 Berlin, Germany.

Historical background: The Berlin TV Tower is a broadcasting tower located in the heart of Berlin. It was built in the late 1960s and is one of the tallest structures in Europe, offering stunning views of the city from its observation deck.

Practical information: The Berlin TV Tower is open daily and admission is charged. Visitors can purchase tickets in advance or at the entrance and can enjoy the views from the observation deck for a fee.

Highlights and must-sees: Visitors can admire the stunning views of Berlin from the observation deck of the Berlin TV Tower, which is one of the tallest structures in Europe.

Cost: Admission to the Berlin TV Tower is charged and prices vary depending on the time of year and type of ticket purchased.

Quality: The Berlin TV Tower is well-maintained and offers a unique and breathtaking experience for visitors looking for panoramic views of Berlin.

Curiosity and facts: The Berlin TV Tower was the first broadcasting tower in East Berlin and remains a landmark of the city's skyline today.

Advice: Visitors should be prepared for long lines, especially during peak tourist season, and should dress appropriately for the weather, as the observation deck is open-air.

Getting there: The Berlin TV Tower is located in the heart of Berlin and is easily accessible by public transportation, including the U-Bahn and S-Bahn.

Nearby attractions: The Brandenburg Gate, Reichstag Building, Berlin Wall Memorial, Berlin Zoo, Pergamon Museum, Museum Island, Berlin Cathedral, Alexanderplatz, and Potsdamer Platz are all within walking distance of the Berlin TV Tower.

SHOPS

KURFÜRSTENDAMM

Address: Kurfürstendamm, 10719 Berlin, Germany.

Phone: +49 30 88710150.

Products: Fashion, beauty, accessories, electronics, home goods, and more.

Hours of operation: Monday-Saturday 10:00 AM to 8:00 PM, Sunday 12:00 PM to 6:00 PM.

Cost score: $$ - $$$

Historical background: Kurfürstendamm, also known as "Ku'damm," is one of the most famous shopping streets in Berlin. It was established in the late 19th century and has been a popular shopping destination ever since. The street has gone through many changes, including being heavily damaged in World War II, but has always remained a hub for shopping and entertainment in the city.

Highlights and must-sees: The Kurfürstendamm is lined with high-end luxury brands, as well as department stores, cafes, and theaters. Some must-visit locations include KaDeWe, Galeries Lafayette, and Quartier 206.

Curiosity and facts: Kurfürstendammis also known for its historical significance as a center of cultural and political life in Berlin. It was a popular gathering place for artists, intellectuals, and political activists in the early 20th century.

Advice: Plan your visit to Kurfürstendamm in advance to make the most of your time and budget. Try to visit on weekdays to avoid the weekend crowds, and be prepared to walk a lot. Dress comfortably and bring cash or credit cards for shopping.

Getting there: Kurfürstendamm can be easily reached by public transportation. Take the U-Bahn to the Uhlandstrasse station or the Wittenbergplatz station, and then walk 5-10 minutes to the street.

Nearby attractions: Some nearby attractions include the Berlin Zoo, the Berlin Wall Memorial, and the Kaiser Wilhelm Memorial Church.

BERLIN CENTRAL STATION

Address: Invalidenstraße 15-17, 10557 Berlin, Germany.

Phone: +49 30 2974600.

Products: Fashion, beauty, accessories, electronics, home goods, and more.

Hours of operation: Monday-Saturday 10:00 AM to 8:00 PM, Sunday 12:00 PM to 6:00 PM.

Cost score: $$ - $$$

Historical background: Berlin Central Station is one of the busiest and largest train stations in Germany. The current building was built in 2006 and replaces the original station that was destroyed during World War II. It serves as a hub for national and international train services, as well as a shopping destination with various stores and restaurants.

Highlights and must-sees: The Berlin Central Station has a variety of shops, ranging from high-end luxury brands to more affordable options. Some must-visit locations include the Alexa Shopping Center and the Bikini Berlin concept mall.

Curiosity and facts: The Berlin Central Station is also known for its modern and environmentally-friendly design, with a green roof and energy-efficient systems. It has become a popular destination for architecture enthusiasts and photographers.

Advice: Plan your visit to Berlin Central Station in advance, especially if you're taking a train and need to make a connection. Make sure to allocate enough time to explore the shopping options and grab a bite to eat. Bring cash or credit cards for shopping.

Getting there: Berlin Central Station is easily accessible by train, bus, or subway. Take the S-Bahn to the Berlin Central Station, or the U-Bahn to the Jannowitzbrücke station and then walk 5-10 minutes to the station.

Nearby attractions: Some nearby attractions include the Museum Island, the Brandenburg Gate, and the Reichstag building.

ALEXA SHOPPING CENTER

Address: Grunerstraße 20, 10179 Berlin, Germany.

Phone: +49 30 290080.

Products: Fashion, beauty, accessories, electronics, home goods, and more.

Hours of operation: Monday-Saturday 10:00 AM to 8:00 PM, Sunday 12:00 PM to 6:00 PM.

Cost score: $$ - $$$

Historical background: Alexa Shopping Center is a large shopping mall located in the heart of Berlin. It opened in 2007 and has since become one of the city's most popular shopping destinations, attracting both locals and tourists.

Highlights and must-sees: Alexa Shopping Center has a wide range of shops, including high-end luxury brands, as well as more affordable options. Some must-visit locations include the H&M store and the Zara store.

Curiosity and facts: Alexa Shopping Center is also known for its modern and innovative design, with a spacious and bright interior. It is a popular destination for those interested in contemporary architecture and design.

Advice: Plan your visit to Alexa Shopping Center in advance to make the most of your time and budget. Make sure to allocate enough time to explore all the shops and grab a bite to eat at one of the many restaurants. Bring cash or credit cards for shopping.

Getting there: Alexa Shopping Center is easily accessible by public transportation. Take the U-Bahn to the Alexanderplatz station, and then walk 5-10 minutes to the mall.

Nearby attractions: Some nearby attractions include the Berlin TV Tower, the Hackescher Markt shopping district, and the Museum Island.

NEUKÖLLN ARCADEN

Address: Karl-Marx-Straße 66, 12043 Berlin, Germany.

Phone: +49 30 683150.

Products: Fashion, beauty, accessories, electronics, home goods, and more.

Hours of operation: Monday-Saturday 10:00 AM to 8:00 PM, Sunday 12:00 PM to 6:00 PM.

Cost score: $ - $$

Historical background: NeuköllnArcaden is a large shopping mall located in the Neuköllnneighborhood of Berlin. It opened in 2008 and has since become a popular shopping destination for locals and tourists alike.

Highlights and must-sees: NeuköllnArcaden offers a variety of shops, ranging from high-end luxury brands to more affordable options. Some must-visit locations include the H&M store and the Zara store.

Curiosity and facts: NeuköllnArcadenis also known for its modern and eco-friendly design, with energy-efficient systems and environmentally-friendly materials. It has become a popular destination for those interested in sustainable architecture and design.

Advice: Plan your visit to NeuköllnArcaden in advance to make the most of your time and budget. Make sure to allocate enough time to explore all the shops and grab a bite to eat at one of the many restaurants. Bring cash or credit cards for shopping.

Getting there: NeuköllnArcaden is easily accessible by public transportation. Take the U-Bahn to the Neukölln station, and then walk 5-10 minutes to the mall.

Nearby attractions: Some nearby attractions include the Tempelhof Park, the Berlin Wall Memorial, and the Neukölln cultural district.

BIKINI BERLIN

Address: Budapester Str. 38-50, 10787 Berlin, Germany.

Phone: +49 30 257680.

Products: Fashion, beauty, accessories, electronics, home goods, and more.

Hours of operation: Monday-Saturday 10:00 AM to 8:00 PM, Sunday 12:00 PM to 6:00 PM.

Cost score: $$ - $$$

Historical background: Bikini Berlin is a shopping and cultural center located in the heart of Berlin. It opened in 2014 and has since become a popular destination for shopping, dining, and entertainment. The center is housed in a unique and modern building that was once part of the Berlin Zoo.

Highlights and must-sees: Bikini Berlin offers a variety of shops, ranging from high-end luxury brands to more affordable options. Some must-visit locations include the Apple store and the Nike store. The center also features a rooftop terrace with views of the city and a variety of restaurants and cafes.

Curiosity and facts: Bikini Berlin is known for its unique and sustainable design, with features such as a green roof and energy-efficient systems. It has become a popular destination for those interested in contemporary architecture and sustainable design.

Advice: Plan your visit to Bikini Berlin in advance to make the most of your time and budget. Make sure to allocate enough time to explore all the shops and enjoy the views from the rooftop terrace. Bring cash or credit cards for shopping.

Getting there: Bikini Berlin is easily accessible by public transportation. Take the U-Bahn to the Zoologischer Garten station, and then walk 5-10 minutes to the center.

Nearby attractions: Some nearby attractions include the Berlin Zoo, the Kaiser Wilhelm Memorial Church, and the Kurfürstendamm shopping street.

GALERIES LAFAYETTE BERLIN

Address: Friedrichstraße 76, 10117 Berlin, Germany.

Phone: +49 30 209470.

Products: Fashion, beauty, accessories, electronics, home goods, and more.

Hours of operation: Monday-Saturday 10:00 AM to 8:00 PM, Sunday 12:00 PM to 6:00 PM.

Cost score: $$ - $$$$

Historical background: Galeries Lafayette Berlin is a luxury department store located in the heart of Berlin. It opened in 2013 and has since become a popular destination for high-end shopping and dining.

Highlights and must-sees: Galeries Lafayette Berlin offers a variety of high-end luxury brands, as well as a gourmet food hall and a rooftop terrace with views of the city. Some must-visit locations include the Chanel store and the Dior store.

Curiosity and facts: Galeries Lafayette Berlin is known for its unique and modern design, with features such as a glass dome and a spacious interior. It has become a popular destination for those interested in contemporary architecture and high-end shopping.

Advice: Plan your visit to Galeries Lafayette Berlin in advance, especially if you're looking to splurge on luxury items. Make sure to allocate enough time to explore all the shops and enjoy the views from the rooftop terrace. Bring cash or credit cards for shopping.

Getting there: Galeries Lafayette Berlin is easily accessible by public transportation. Take the U-Bahn to the Friedrichstraße station, and then walk 5-10 minutes to the store.

Nearby attractions: Some nearby attractions include the Brandenburg Gate, the Reichstag building, and the Museum Island.

QUARTIER 206

Address: Friedrichstraße 71, 10117 Berlin, Germany.

Phone: +49 30 206780.

Products: Fashion, beauty, accessories, home goods, and more.

Hours of operation: Monday-Saturday 10:00 AM to 8:00 PM, Sunday 12:00 PM to 6:00 PM.

Cost score: $$ - $$$

Historical background: Quartier 206 is a luxury shopping center located in the heart of Berlin. It opened in 2009 and has since become a popular destination for high-end shopping and dining.

Highlights and must-sees: Quartier 206 offers a variety of high-end luxury brands, as well as a gourmet food hall and a rooftop terrace with views of the city. Some must-visit locations include the Gucci store and the Prada store.

Curiosity and facts: Quartier 206 is known for its unique and modern design, with features such as a spacious interior and a glass atrium. It has become a popular destination for those interested in contemporary architecture and high-end shopping.

Advice: Plan your visit to Quartier 206 in advance, especially if you're looking to splurge on luxury items. Make sure to allocate enough time to explore all the shops and enjoy the views from the rooftop terrace. Bring cash or credit cards for shopping.

Getting there: Quartier 206 is easily accessible by public transportation. Take the U-Bahn to the Friedrichstraße station, and then walk 5-10 minutes to the center.

Nearby attractions: Some nearby attractions include the Brandenburg Gate, the Reichstag building, and the Museum Island.

KADEWE

Address: Tauentzienstraße 21-24, 10789 Berlin, Germany.

Phone: +49 30 21120.

Products: Fashion, beauty, accessories, electronics, home goods, and more.

Hours of operation: Monday-Saturday 10:00 AM to 8:00 PM, Sunday 12:00 PM to 6:00 PM.

Cost score: $$ - $$$$

Historical background: KADEWE is a luxury department store located in the heart of Berlin. It opened in 1907 and has since become one of the city's most popular shopping destinations, attracting both locals and tourists.

Highlights and must-sees: KADEWE offers a variety of high-end luxury brands, as well as a gourmet food hall and a rooftop terrace with views of the city. Some must-visit locations include the Hermès store and the Louis Vuitton store.

Curiosity and facts: KADEWE is known for its elegant and spacious interior, and is considered one of the largest department stores in Europe. It has a long history in Berlin and has become a cultural icon of the city.

Advice: Plan your visit to KADEWE in advance, especially if you're looking to splurge on luxury items. Make sure to allocate enough time to explore all the shops and enjoy the views from the rooftop terrace. Bring cash or credit cards for shopping.

Getting there: KADEWE is easily accessible by public transportation. Take the U-Bahn to the Wittenbergplatz station, and then walk 5-10 minutes to the store.

Nearby attractions: Some nearby attractions include the KaDeWe Group, the Kurfürstendamm shopping street, and the Berlin Zoo.

MALL OF BERLIN

Address: Leipziger Platz 12, 10117 Berlin, Germany.

Phone: +49 30 209480.

Products: Fashion, beauty, accessories, electronics, home goods, and more.

Hours of operation: Monday-Saturday 10:00 AM to 8:00 PM, Sunday 12:00 PM to 6:00 PM.

Cost score: $ - $$

Historical background: Mall of Berlin is a large shopping mall located in the heart of Berlin. It opened in 2014 and has since become a popular shopping destination for locals and tourists alike.

Highlights and must-sees: Mall of Berlin offers a variety of shops, ranging from high-end luxury brands to more affordable options. Some must-visit locations include the H&M store and the Zara store.

Curiosity and facts: Mall of Berlin is also known for its modern and eco-friendly design, with energy-efficient systems and environmentally-friendly materials. It has become a popular destination for those interested in sustainable architecture and design.

Advice: Plan your visit to Mall of Berlin in advance to make the most of your time and budget. Make sure to allocate enough time to explore all the shops and grab a bite to eat at one of the many restaurants. Bring cash or credit cards for shopping.

Getting there: Mall of Berlin is easily accessible by public transportation. Take the U-Bahn to the Leipziger Platz station, and then walk 5-10 minutes to the mall.

Nearby attractions: Some nearby attractions include the Potsdamer Platz, the Brandenburg Gate, and the Reichstag building.

BERLINER FREIHEIT

Address: Kurfürstendamm 216, 10719 Berlin, Germany.

Phone: +49 30 887110.

Products: Fashion, beauty, accessories, home goods, and more.

Hours of operation: Monday-Saturday 10:00 AM to 8:00 PM, Sunday 12:00 PM to 6:00 PM.

Cost score: $$ - $$$

Historical background: Berliner Freiheit is a shopping center located in the heart of Berlin. It opened in the 1990s and has since become a popular destination for shopping and dining.

Highlights and must-sees: Berliner Freiheit offers a variety of shops, ranging from high-end luxury brands to more affordable options. Some must-visit locations include the Chanel store and the Gucci store.

Curiosity and facts: Berliner Freiheit is known for its central location and easy access to other popular attractions in Berlin. It is also a popular destination for those interested in contemporary architecture and design.

Advice: Plan your visit to Berliner Freiheit in advance to make the most of your time and budget. Make sure to allocate enough time to explore all the shops and grab a bite to eat at one of the many restaurants. Bring cash or credit cards for shopping.

Getting there: Berliner Freiheit is easily accessible by public transportation. Take the U-Bahn to the Kurfürstendamm station, and then walk 5-10 minutes to the center.

Nearby attractions: Some nearby attractions include the Kurfürstendamm shopping street, the Berlin Zoo, and the Kaiser Wilhelm Memorial Church.

MUSEUMS

PERGAMON MUSEUM

Address: Am Kupfergraben 5, 10117 Berlin, Germany.

Phone: +49 30 2090-5577

Exhibitions and collections: The Pergamon Museum displays monumental structures such as the Pergamon Altar and the Ishtar Gate of Babylon, as well as the Market Gate of Miletus and the Mshatta Facade. It also has a collection of Islamic art.

Admission fees and hours of operation: The museum is open from Tuesday to Sunday, from 10:00 AM to 6:00 PM. The admission fee is 12€ for adults and 6€ for concessions.

Historical background: The Pergamon Museum was built in 1930 and is one of the largest museums in Germany. It was built to house the architectural treasures of the ancient city of Pergamon.

Highlights and must-sees: The Pergamon Altar, the Ishtar Gate of Babylon, the Market Gate of Miletus, the Mshatta Facade, and the Islamic art collection are some of the most famous exhibits of the museum.

Curiosity and facts: The Pergamon Altar, which is one of the most famous exhibits of the museum, was built in the 2nd century BC in the ancient city of Pergamon.

Advice: Visitors should allow at least 2-3 hours to fully explore the museum.

Getting there: The Pergamon Museum is located near the Berlin Friedrichstraße railway station. From there, visitors can take the U6 metro line to the FranzösischeStraße station, which is just a 5-minute walk from the museum.

Nearby attractions: The Berlin Cathedral, the New National Gallery, and the Museum Island are some of the nearby attractions that visitors can explore after visiting the Pergamon Museum.

MUSEUM ISLAND

Address: Museum Island, Berlin, Germany.

Phone: +49 30 2090-5577

Exhibitions and collections: Museum Island houses five of Berlin's most important museums: the Alte Nationalgalerie, the Alte Museum, the Bode Museum, the Pergamon Museum, and the Neues Museum. It showcases a range of exhibits, including classical antiquities, Byzantine art, and German art from the 19th century.

Admission fees and hours of operation: The Museum Island is open from Tuesday to Sunday, from 10:00 AM to 6:00 PM. The admission fee varies depending on the museum.

Historical background: Museum Island was designated a UNESCO World Heritage Site in 1999. It was originally built in the 19th century to house the royal collections of Prussian kings and to serve as a center for scientific and cultural research.

Highlights and must-sees: The Alte Nationalgalerie, the Alte Museum, the Bode Museum, the Pergamon Museum, and the Neues Museum are some of the must-sees on Museum Island.

Curiosity and facts: Museum Island is one of the largest museum complexes in the world and is considered one of Berlin's top tourist attractions.

Advice: Visitors should plan ahead and allow enough time to visit all five museums on Museum Island.

Getting there: Museum Island is located in the center of Berlin and can be easily reached by public transportation. Visitors can take the S-Bahn or U-Bahn to the Alexanderplatz station and then walk to the island.

Nearby attractions: The Berlin Cathedral, the Friedrichstraße shopping street, and the Brandenburg Gate are some of the nearby attractions that visitors can explore after visiting Museum Island.

JEWISH MUSEUM BERLIN

Address: Lindenstraße 9-14, 10969 Berlin, Germany.

Phone: +49 30 25993-300

Exhibitions and collections: The Jewish Museum Berlin showcases the history of Jewish life in Germany, from the Middle Ages to the present day. It features a range of exhibits, including historical artifacts, photographs, and interactive displays.

Admission fees and hours of operation: The museum is open from Monday to Sunday, from 10:00 AM to 8:00 PM. The admission fee is 8€ for adults and 4€ for concessions.

Historical background: The Jewish Museum Berlin was opened in 2001 and is one of the largest Jewish museums in Europe. It was built to commemorate the rich cultural heritage of Jews in Germany and to educate the public about the history of Jewish life in the country.

Highlights and must-sees: The permanent exhibitions, the Garden of Exile, and the Holocaust Tower are some of the must-sees at the Jewish Museum Berlin.

Curiosity and facts: The Jewish Museum Berlin was designed by the famous architect Daniel Libeskind and is considered one of the city's most important cultural institutions.

Advice: Visitors should allow at least 2 hours to fully explore the museum.

Getting there: The Jewish Museum Berlin is located near the Berlin Nordbahnhof railway station. Visitors can take the U-Bahn to the Hallesches Tor station, which is just a 5-minute walk from the museum.

Nearby attractions: The Berlin Wall Memorial, the Checkpoint Charlie Museum, and the Topography of Terror are some of the nearby attractions that visitors can explore after visiting the Jewish Museum Berlin.

DDR MUSEUM

Address: Karl-Liebknecht-Straße 1, 10178 Berlin, Germany.

Phone: +49 30 847123770

Exhibitions and collections: The DDR Museum showcases the history and everyday life of East Germany, also known as the German Democratic Republic (GDR). It features a range of exhibits, including original GDR artifacts, interactive displays, and multimedia presentations.

Admission fees and hours of operation: The museum is open from Monday to Sunday, from 10:00 AM to 8:00 PM. The admission fee is 12€ for adults and 6€ for concessions.

Historical background: The DDR Museum was opened in 2006 and is one of the few museums in the world dedicated to the history and culture of East Germany.

Highlights and must-sees: The interactive exhibits, the original GDR artifacts, and the multimedia presentations are some of the must-sees at the DDR Museum.

Curiosity and facts: The DDR Museum is a highly interactive museum and is designed to give visitors a hands-on experience of life in East Germany.

Advice: Visitors should allow at least 1 hour to fully explore the museum.

Getting there: The DDR Museum is located near the Berlin Alexanderplatz railway station. Visitors can take the U-Bahn to the Alexanderplatz station, which is just a 5-minute walk from the museum.

Nearby attractions: The Berlin Wall Memorial, the Checkpoint Charlie Museum, and the Topography of Terror are some of the nearby attractions that visitors can explore after visiting the DDR Museum.

BERLIN WALL MUSEUM

Address: Bernauer Straße 111, 13355 Berlin, Germany.

Phone: +49 30 46798-0

Exhibitions and collections: The Berlin Wall Museum showcases the history of the Berlin Wall, from its construction in 1961 to its fall in 1989. It features a range of exhibits, including original artifacts, photographs, and interactive displays.

Admission fees and hours of operation: The museum is open from Monday to Sunday, from 10:00 AM to 8:00 PM. The admission fee is 8€ for adults and 4€ for concessions.

Historical background: The Berlin Wall Museum was opened in 2006 and is dedicated to the history of the Berlin Wall and its impact on the city and its residents.

Highlights and must-sees: The original Berlin Wall artifacts, the interactive displays, and the historical photographs are some of the must-sees at the Berlin Wall Museum.

Curiosity and facts: The Berlin Wall Museum is located on Bernauer Straße, which was one of the most iconic and heavily guarded sections of the Berlin Wall.

Advice: Visitors should allow at least 1 hour to fully explore the museum.

Getting there: The Berlin Wall Museum is located near the Berlin Nordbahnhof railway station. Visitors can take the U-Bahn to the Bernauer Straße station, which is just a 5-minute walk from the museum.

Nearby attractions: The Berlin Wall Memorial, Checkpoint Charlie Museum, and the Topography of Terror are some of the nearby attractions that visitors can explore after visiting the Berlin Wall Museum.

MUSEUM OF NATURAL HISTORY

Address: Invalidenstraße 43, 10115 Berlin, Germany.

Phone: +49 30 2093-8973

Exhibitions and collections: The Museum of Natural History showcases a wide range of specimens and specimens from the natural world, including fossils, minerals, and animal specimens. It also features interactive displays and multimedia presentations.

Admission fees and hours of operation: The museum is open from Tuesday to Sunday, from 10:00 AM to 6:00 PM. The admission fee is 8€ for adults and 4€ for concessions.

Historical background: The Museum of Natural History was established in 1810 and is one of the largest natural history museums in the world.

Highlights and must-sees: The dinosaur exhibits, the mineral collections, and the interactive displays are some of the must-sees at the Museum of Natural History.

Curiosity and facts: The Museum of Natural History is home to one of the largest collections of dinosaur fossils in the world.

Advice: Visitors should allow at least 2 hours to fully explore the museum.

Getting there: The Museum of Natural History is located near the Berlin Hauptbahnhof railway station. Visitors can take the S-Bahn to the Friedrichstraße station, which is just a 10-minute walk from the museum.

Nearby attractions: The Berlin Zoo, the Berlin Cathedral, and the New National Gallery are some of the nearby attractions that visitors can explore after visiting the Museum of Natural History.

DEUTSCHES TECHNIKMUSEUM

Address: TrebbinerStraße 9, 10963 Berlin, Germany.

Phone: +49 30 90210-0

Exhibitions and collections: The DeutschesTechnikmuseumshowcases the history of technology and science in Germany, from the Middle Ages to the present day. It features a range of exhibits, including historical artifacts, interactive displays, and multimedia presentations.

Admission fees and hours of operation: The museum is open from Tuesday to Sunday, from 10:00 AM to 6:00 PM. The admission fee is 8€ for adults and 4€ for concessions.

Historical background: The DeutschesTechnikmuseum was founded in 1982 and is one of the largest technology museums in the world.

Highlights and must-sees: The exhibits on transportation, energy, and communication are some of the must-sees at the DeutschesTechnikmuseum.

Curiosity and facts: The DeutschesTechnikmuseumis home to one of the largest collections of historical aircraft in Europe.

Advice: Visitors should allow at least 2 hours to fully explore the museum.

Getting there: The DeutschesTechnikmuseum is located near the Berlin Ostbahnhof railway station. Visitors can take the S-Bahn to the Ostbahnhof station, which is just a 5-minute walk from the museum.

Nearby attractions: The Berlin Wall Memorial, Checkpoint Charlie Museum, and the New National Gallery are some of the nearby attractions that visitors can explore after visiting the DeutschesTechnikmuseum.

TOPOGRAPHY OF TERROR

Address: Niederkirchnerstraße 8, 10963 Berlin, Germany.

Phone: +49 30 254509-50

Exhibitions and collections: The Topography of Terror is a museum and documentation center dedicated to the history of the Nazi regime and the Gestapo, the secret police of Nazi Germany. It features a range of exhibits, including historical artifacts, photographs, and interactive displays.

Admission fees and hours of operation: The museum is open from Tuesday to Sunday, from 10:00 AM to 6:00 PM. Admission is free.

Historical background: The Topography of Terror was established in 2010 on the site of the former Gestapo and SS headquarters in Berlin.

Highlights and must-sees: The outdoor exhibitions, the historical photographs, and the interactive displays are some of the must-sees at the Topography of Terror.

Curiosity and facts: The Topography of Terror is considered one of the most important historical sites in Berlin, and is a must-visit for anyone interested in the history of the Nazi regime and the Gestapo.

Advice: Visitors should allow at least 1 hour to fully explore the museum.

Getting there: The Topography of Terror is located near the Berlin Potsdamer Platz railway station. Visitors can take the U-Bahn to the Potsdamer Platz station, which is just a 10-minute walk from the museum.

Nearby attractions: The Brandenburg Gate, the Reichstag building, and Checkpoint Charlie Museum are some of the nearby attractions that visitors can explore after visiting the Topography of Terror.

NEW NATIONAL GALLERY

Address: Potsdamer Straße 50, 10785 Berlin, Germany.

Phone: +49 30 2662951

Exhibitions and collections: The New National Gallery showcases modern and contemporary art, including works by famous artists such as Pablo Picasso, Max Ernst, and Jackson Pollock. It features a range of exhibits, including paintings, sculptures, and multimedia presentations.

Admission fees and hours of operation: The museum is open from Tuesday to Sunday, from 10:00 AM to 6:00 PM. The admission fee is 10€ for adults and 5€ for concessions.

Historical background: The New National Gallery was established in 1968 and is dedicated to modern and contemporary art.

Highlights and must-sees: The exhibitions on modern art, the sculptures, and the multimedia presentations are some of the must-sees at the New National Gallery.

Curiosity and facts: The New National Gallery is home to one of the largest collections of modern and contemporary art in Europe.

Advice: Visitors should allow at least 2 hours to fully explore the museum.

Getting there: The New National Gallery is located near the Berlin Potsdamer Platz railway station. Visitors can take the U-Bahn to the Potsdamer Platz station, which is just a 5-minute walk from the museum.

Nearby attractions: The Brandenburg Gate, the Reichstag building, and the Topography of Terror are some of the nearby attractions that visitors can explore after visiting the New National Gallery.

MUSEUM FÜR FOTOGRAFIE

Address: Jebensstraße 2, 10623 Berlin, Germany.

Phone: +49 30 330069-0

Exhibitions and collections: The Museum für Fotografieshowcases the history of photography, from its origins to the present day. It features a range of exhibits, including photographs, historical artifacts, and interactive displays.

Admission fees and hours of operation: The museum is open from Tuesday to Sunday, from 10:00 AM to 6:00 PM. The admission fee is 8€ for adults and 4€ for concessions.

Historical background: The Museum für Fotografie was established in 2004 and is dedicated to the history and art of photography.

Highlights and must-sees: The exhibits on the history of photography, the historical artifacts, and the interactive displays are some of the must-sees at the Museum für Fotografie.

Curiosity and facts: The Museum für Fotografie is home to one of the largest collections of historical photographs in Europe.

Advice: Visitors should allow at least 1 hour to fully explore the museum.

Getting there: The Museum für Fotografie is located near the Berlin Zoo railway station. Visitors can take the U-Bahn to the Zoo station, which is just a 5-minute walk from the museum.

Nearby attractions: The Berlin Zoo, the Berlin Cathedral, and the Museum of Natural History are some of the nearby attractions that visitors can explore after visiting the Museum für Fotografie.

THEATERS

BERLIN STATE OPERA

Address: Unter den Linden 7, 10117 Berlin, Germany.

Phone: +49 30 2035 88250.

Performances and shows: Ballet, classical music, and opera performances.

Ticket prices and availability: Ticket prices vary depending on the performance and seat location, and tickets can be purchased online or at the box office.

Show times: Performances are held in the evenings, typically starting at 7:00pm or 8:00pm, with some matinee performances on weekends.

Historical background: The Berlin State Opera was founded in 1693 and has a long history of producing world-class performances. It was heavily damaged during World War II, but was restored and reopened in 1955.

Highlights and must-sees: Don't miss the famous productions of "The Magic Flute" and "Swan Lake".

Curiosity and facts: The Berlin State Opera is one of the leading opera houses in the world, and has been home to many famous musicians, including composer Richard Strauss.

Advice: Arrive early to enjoy a drink in the historic opera bar before the performance starts.

Getting there: The Berlin State Opera is located in the Mitte neighborhood, and can be reached by taking the U-Bahn line U2 to the "Unter den Linden" station, or by taking the S-Bahn line S5, S7, or S75 to the "Friedrichstraße" station.

Nearby attractions: The Berlin State Opera is located near the Brandenburg Gate, the Reichstag building, and the Museum Island.

DEUTSCHES THEATER

Address: Schumannstraße 13a, 10117 Berlin, Germany.

Phone: +49 30 2844 1233.

Performances and shows: Drama, comedy, and musical performances.

Ticket prices and availability: Ticket prices vary depending on the performance and seat location, and tickets can be purchased online or at the box office.

Show times: Performances are held in the evenings, typically starting at 7:00pm or 8:00pm, with some matinee performances on weekends.

Historical background: The DeutschesTheater was founded in 1850 and is one of the oldest theaters in Berlin. It has a rich history of producing world-class performances and has been home to many famous actors and playwrights.

Highlights and must-sees: Don't miss the famous productions of "Hamlet" and "Theater of Blood".

Curiosity and facts: The DeutschesTheater was heavily damaged during World War II, but was restored and reopened in 1951. It is considered one of the most important theaters in Germany.

Advice: Arrive early to enjoy a drink in the theater bar before the performance starts.

Getting there: The DeutschesTheater is located in the Mitte neighborhood, and can be reached by taking the U-

Bahn line U2 to the "Stadtmitte" station, or by taking the S-Bahn line S5, S7, or S75 to the "Friedrichstraße" station.

Nearby attractions: The DeutschesTheater is located near the Brandenburg Gate, the Reichstag building, and the Museum Island.

BERLINER ENSEMBLE

Address: Bertolt-Brecht-Platz 1, 10117 Berlin, Germany.

Phone: +49 30 4799 7499.

Performances and shows: Drama and musical performances.

Ticket prices and availability: Ticket prices vary depending on the performance and seat location, and tickets can be purchased online or at the box office.

Show times: Performances are held in the evenings, typically starting at 7:00pm or 8:00pm, with some matinee performances on weekends.

Historical background: The Berliner Ensemble was founded in 1949 by playwright Bertolt Brecht and his wife Helene Weigel. It has a rich history of producing politically and socially engaged performances and has been home to many famous actors and playwrights.

Highlights and must-sees: Don't miss the famous productions of "The Threepenny Opera" and "Mother Courage and Her Children".

Curiosity and facts: The Berliner Ensemble is considered one of the most important theaters in Germany and has a strong tradition of political and social engagement in its performances.

Advice: Arrive early to enjoy a drink in the theater bar before the performance starts.

Getting there: The Berliner Ensemble is located in the Mitte neighborhood, and can be reached by taking the U-Bahn line U2 to the "Stadtmitte" station, or by taking the S-Bahn line S5, S7, or S75 to the "Friedrichstraße" station.

Nearby attractions: The Berliner Ensemble is located near the Brandenburg Gate, the Reichstag building, and the Museum Island.

KOMISCHE OPER BERLIN

Address: Behrenstraße 55-57, 10117 Berlin, Germany.

Phone: +49 30 4799 7499.

Performances and shows: Opera, operetta, and musical performances.

Ticket prices and availability: Ticket prices vary depending on the performance and seat location, and tickets can be purchased online or at the box office.

Show times: Performances are held in the evenings, typically starting at 7:00pm or 8:00pm, with some matinee performances on weekends.

Historical background: The Komische Oper Berlin was founded in 1947 and has a long history of producing opera, operetta, and musical performances. It is known for its innovative and modern productions.

Highlights and must-sees: Don't miss the famous productions of "The Barber of Seville" and "The Magic Flute".

Curiosity and facts: The Komische Oper Berlin is one of the leading opera houses in Germany, and is known for its innovative and modern productions.

Advice: Arrive early to enjoy a drink in the theater bar before the performance starts.

Getting there: The Komische Oper Berlin is located in the Mitte neighborhood, and can be reached by taking the U-Bahn line U2 to the "Stadtmitte" station, or by taking the S-Bahn line S5, S7, or S75 to the "Hackescher Markt" station.

Nearby attractions: The Komische Oper Berlin is located near the Brandenburg Gate, the Reichstag building, and the Museum Island.

MAXIM GORKI THEATER

Address: Am Festungsgraben 2, 10117 Berlin, Germany.

Phone: +49 30 20221 123.

Performances and shows: Drama and musical performances.

Ticket prices and availability: Ticket prices vary depending on the performance and seat location, and tickets can be purchased online or at the box office.

Show times: Performances are held in the evenings, typically starting at 7:00pm or 8:00pm, with some matinee performances on weekends.

Historical background: The Maxim Gorki Theater was founded in 1984 and has a long history of producing politically and socially engaged performances. It is named after the famous Russian writer and playwright Maxim Gorky.

Highlights and must-sees: Don't miss the famous productions of "The Lower Depths" and "The Mother".

Curiosity and facts: The Maxim Gorki Theater is one of the most important theaters in Germany and has a strong tradition of political and social engagement in its performances.

Advice: Arrive early to enjoy a drink in the theater bar before the performance starts.

Getting there: The Maxim Gorki Theater is located in the Mitte neighborhood, and can be reached by taking the U-Bahn line U5 to the "Alexanderplatz" station, or by taking the S-Bahn line S5, S7, or S75 to the "Friedrichstraße" station.

Nearby attractions: The Maxim Gorki Theater is located near the Berlin Wall Memorial, the Berlin TV Tower, and the Nikolaiviertelneighborhood.

SCHAUBÜHNE BERLIN

Address: Kurfürstendamm 153, 10719 Berlin, Germany.

Phone: +49 30 8863 7980.

Performances and shows: Drama and musical performances.

Ticket prices and availability: Ticket prices vary depending on the performance and seat location, and tickets can be purchased online or at the box office.

Show times: Performances are held in the evenings, typically starting at 7:00pm or 8:00pm, with some matinee performances on weekends.

Historical background: The Schaubühne Berlin was founded in 1962 and has a long history of producing innovative and modern performances. It is considered one of the most important theaters in Germany.

Highlights and must-sees: Don't miss the famous productions of "Hamlet" and "The Glass Menagerie".

Curiosity and facts: The Schaubühne Berlin is known for its bold and innovative productions, and has been home to many famous directors and actors.

Advice: Arrive early to enjoy a drink in the theater bar before the performance starts.

Getting there: The Schaubühne Berlin is located in the Charlottenburg neighborhood, and can be reached by taking the U-Bahn line U7 to the "Savignyplatz" station, or by taking the S-Bahn line S41, S42, S45, or S46 to the "Charlottenburg" station.

Nearby attractions: The Schaubühne Berlin is located near the Kurfürstendamm shopping street, the Zoo Berlin, and the Charlottenburg Palace.

KONZERTHAUS BERLIN

Address: Gendarmenmarkt, 10117 Berlin, Germany.

Phone: +49 30 2030 940.

Performances and shows: Classical music, jazz, and world music performances.

Ticket prices and availability: Ticket prices vary depending on the performance and seat location, and tickets can be purchased online or at the box office.

Show times: Performances are held in the evenings and afternoons, with show times varying depending on the performance.

Historical background: The Konzerthaus Berlin was built in 1821 and has a long history of hosting classical music performances. It has undergone several renovations and restorations over the years, and is now considered one of the premier concert venues in Germany.

Highlights and must-sees: Don't miss the famous concerts by the Berlin Philharmonic Orchestra and the Chamber Music Festival Berlin.

Curiosity and facts: The Konzerthaus Berlin is known for its exceptional acoustics and stunning neoclassical architecture, making it a favorite venue for musicians and music lovers alike.

Advice: Arrive early to enjoy a drink in the theater bar before the performance starts.

Getting there: The Konzerthaus Berlin is located in the Mitte neighborhood, and can be reached by taking the U-Bahn line U2 to the "Stadtmitte" station, or by taking the S-Bahn line S5, S7, or S75 to the "Friedrichstraße" station.

Nearby attractions: The Konzerthaus Berlin is located near the Gendarmenmarkt square, the Brandenburg Gate, and the Reichstag building.

BERLINER PHILHARMONIE

Address: Herbert-von-Karajan-Straße 1, 10785 Berlin, Germany.

Phone: +49 30 254 88 999.

Performances and shows: Classical music, jazz, and world music performances.

Ticket prices and availability: Ticket prices vary depending on the performance and seat location, and tickets can be purchased online or at the box office.

Show times: Performances are held in the evenings and afternoons, with show times varying depending on the performance.

Historical background: The Berliner Philharmonie was built in 1963 and is the home of the Berlin Philharmonic Orchestra. It is considered one of the finest concert halls in the world and has hosted many famous musicians and performances over the years.

Highlights and must-sees: Don't miss the famous concerts by the Berlin Philharmonic Orchestra and the Chamber Music Festival Berlin.

Curiosity and facts: The Berliner Philharmonic is known for its exceptional acoustics and modern architecture, making it a favorite venue for musicians and music lovers alike.

Advice: Arrive early to enjoy a drink in the theater bar before the performance starts.

Getting there: The Berliner Philharmonie is located in the Tiergarten neighborhood, and can be reached by taking the U-Bahn line U2 to the "Potsdamer Platz" station, or by taking the S-Bahn line S1, S2, or S25 to the "Potsdamer Platz" station.

Nearby attractions: The Berliner Philharmonie is located near the Potsdamer Platz square, the Brandenburg Gate, and the Memorial to the Murdered Jews of Europe.

FRIEDRICHSTADT-PALAST

Address: Friedrichstraße 107, 10117 Berlin, Germany.

Phone: +49 30 2326 2326.

Performances and shows: Variety shows, musicals, and revues.

Ticket prices and availability: Ticket prices vary depending on the performance and seat location, and tickets can be purchased online or at the box office.

Show times: Performances are held in the evenings, typically starting at 7:00pm or 8:00pm, with some matinee performances on weekends.

Historical background: The Friedrichstadt-Palast was founded in the 19th century and is one of the oldest and most famous variety theaters in Germany. It has undergone several renovations and restorations over the years and is now considered one of the premier theaters for variety shows in Europe.

Highlights and must-sees: Don't miss the famous productions of "The One Grand Show" and "Berlin - The Show".

Curiosity and facts: The Friedrichstadt-Palast is known for its grand stage, elaborate costumes, and exceptional performers, making it a favorite venue for variety shows and revues.

Advice: Arrive early to enjoy a drink in the theater bar before the performance starts.

Getting there: The Friedrichstadt-Palast is located in the Mitte neighborhood, and can be reached by taking the U-Bahn line U2 to the "Stadtmitte" station, or by taking the S-Bahn line S5, S7, or S75 to the "Friedrichstraße" station.

Nearby attractions: The Friedrichstadt-Palast is located near the Checkpoint Charlie Museum, the Berlin Wall Memorial, and the Nikolaiviertelneighborhood.

HAUS DER BERLINER FESTSPIELE

Address: Schaperstraße 24, 10719 Berlin, Germany.

Phone: +49 30 254 89 100.

Performances and shows: Dance, theater, music, and multimedia performances.

Ticket prices and availability: Ticket prices vary depending on the performance and seat location, and tickets can be purchased online or at the box office.

Show times: Performances are held in the evenings and afternoons, with show times varying depending on the performance.

Historical background: The Haus der Berliner Festspiele was built in the 1960s and is the main venue for the Berlin Festival. It is considered one of the premier cultural venues in Berlin, and has hosted many important dance, theater, music, and multimedia performances over the years.

Highlights and must-sees: Don't miss the famous productions of "The Nutcracker" and "Romeo and Juliet".

Curiosity and facts: The Haus der Berliner Festspiele is known for its exceptional acoustics and modern architecture, making it a favorite venue for performing artists and audiences alike.

Advice: Arrive early to enjoy a drink in the theater bar before the performance starts.

Getting there: The Haus der Berliner Festspiele is located in the Wilmersdorf neighborhood, and can be reached by taking the U-Bahn line U3 to the "Savignyplatz" station, or by taking the S-Bahn line S41, S42, S45, or S46 to the "Charlottenburg" station.

Nearby attractions: The Haus der Berliner Festspiele is located near the Kurfürstendamm shopping street, the Zoo Berlin, and the Charlottenburg Palace.

GALLERIES

NATIONALGALERIE

Address: Bodestraße 1-3, 10178 Berlin, Germany

Phone: +49 30 266 42 42 42

Exhibitions and collections: The Nationalgalerie Berlin showcases a diverse range of art from the 19th to the 21st century, including works by Caspar David Friedrich, Auguste Rodin, Pablo Picasso, and Gerhard Richter.

Admission fees and hours of operation: Admission is free, and the museum is open from Tuesday to Sunday, 10:00am to 6:00pm.

Historical background: The Nationalgalerie Berlin was founded in 1961, and has since become one of the most important art museums in Germany, showcasing works from the 19th to the 21st century.

Highlights and must-sees: Some of the must-see works at Nationalgalerie Berlin include Caspar David Friedrich's "Wanderer Above the Sea of Fog," Pablo Picasso's "Les Demoiselles d'Avignon," and Gerhard Richter's "October 18, 1977."

Curiosity and facts: The Nationalgalerie Berlin is one of the largest art museums in Germany, and is home to over 20,000 works of art.

Advice: To fully enjoy your visit to the Nationalgalerie Berlin, it's best to plan ahead and decide which exhibitions and collections you want to see, as there is a lot of ground to cover in this large museum.

Getting there: The Nationalgalerie Berlin is easily accessible by public transportation, and is located near the Friedrichstraße metro station. From there, simply take the U6 line and get off at the Oranienburger Tor stop. The museum is located a short walk from the station.

Nearby attractions: Some of the nearby attractions to the Nationalgalerie Berlin include the Berlin Wall Memorial, the Checkpoint Charlie Museum, and the New National Gallery.

HAMBURGER BAHNHOF

Address: Invalidenstraße 50-51, 10557 Berlin, Germany

Phone: +49 30 3978 3411

Exhibitions and collections: Hamburger Bahnhof is a contemporary art museum that showcases works by some of the most influential artists of the 20th and 21st centuries, including Pablo Picasso, Cy Twombly, and Gerhard Richter.

Admission fees and hours of operation: Admission is free, and the museum is open from Tuesday to Sunday, 10:00am to 6:00pm.

Historical background: Hamburger Bahnhof was opened in 1996, and has since become one of the most important contemporary art museums in Germany, exhibiting works by some of the most influential artists of the 20th and 21st centuries.

Highlights and must-sees: Some of the must-see works at Hamburger Bahnhof include Pablo Picasso's "Les Demoiselles d'Avignon," Cy Twombly's "Untitled (Rome)," and Gerhard Richter's "October 18, 1977."

Curiosity and facts: Hamburger Bahnhof is housed in a former train station, giving it a unique and historical setting for contemporary art exhibitions.

Advice: To fully enjoy your visit to Hamburger Bahnhof, be sure to spend some time exploring the museum's exhibitions and collections, as well as its unique architectural features.

Getting there: Hamburger Bahnhof is easily accessible by public transportation, and is located near the Nordbahnhof metro station. From there, simply take the S1, S2, or S25 line and get off at the Hauptbahnhof stop. The museum is located a short walk from the station.

Nearby attractions: Some of the nearby attractions to Hamburger Bahnhof include the Berlin Wall Memorial, the Checkpoint Charlie Museum, and the New National Gallery.

CONTEMPORARY FINE ARTS

Address: Auguststraße 50, 10117 Berlin, Germany

Phone: +49 30 280 96 96 0

Exhibitions and collections: Contemporary Fine Arts is a contemporary art gallery that showcases works by some of the most influential artists of the 20th and 21st centuries, including Pablo Picasso, Cy Twombly, and Gerhard Richter.

Admission fees and hours of operation: Admission is free, and the gallery is open from Tuesday to Saturday, 11:00am to 6:00pm.

Historical background: Contemporary Fine Arts was founded in 1984, and has since become one of the most important contemporary art galleries in Germany, exhibiting works by some of the most influential artists of the 20th and 21st centuries.

Highlights and must-sees: Some of the must-see works at Contemporary Fine Arts include Pablo Picasso's "Les Demoiselles d'Avignon," Cy Twombly's "Untitled (Rome)," and Gerhard Richter's "October 18, 1977."

Curiosity and facts: Contemporary Fine Arts is known for its innovative exhibitions and its commitment to showcasing the works of up-and-coming artists.

Advice: To fully enjoy your visit to Contemporary Fine Arts, be sure to spend some time exploring the gallery's exhibitions and collections, and to ask the knowledgeable staff for recommendations on which artists and works to see.

Getting there: Contemporary Fine Arts is easily accessible by public transportation, and is located near the Oranienburger Tor metro station. From there, simply take the U6 line and get off at the Oranienburger Tor stop. The gallery is located a short walk from the station.

Nearby attractions: Some of the nearby attractions to Contemporary Fine Arts include the Berlin Wall Memorial, the Checkpoint Charlie Museum, and the New National Gallery.

GALERIE EIGEN + ART

Address: Auguststraße 26, 10117 Berlin, Germany

Phone: +49 30 280 986 60

Exhibitions and collections: Galerie Eigen + Art is a contemporary art gallery that showcases works by some of the most influential artists of the 20th and 21st centuries, including Pablo Picasso, Cy Twombly, and Gerhard Richter.

Admission fees and hours of operation: Admission is free, and the gallery is open from Tuesday to Saturday, 11:00am to 6:00pm.

Historical background: Galerie Eigen + Art was founded in Leipzig in 1985, and has since become one of the most important contemporary art galleries in Germany, exhibiting works by some of the most influential artists of the 20th and 21st centuries.

Highlights and must-sees: Some of the must-see works at Galerie Eigen + Art include Pablo Picasso's "Les Demoiselles d'Avignon," Cy Twombly's "Untitled (Rome)," and Gerhard Richter's "October 18, 1977."

Curiosity and facts: Galerie Eigen + Art is known for its focus on contemporary art and its commitment to showcasing the works of up-and-coming artists.

Advice: To fully enjoy your visit to Galerie Eigen + Art, be sure to spend some time exploring the gallery's exhibitions and collections, and to ask the knowledgeable staff for recommendations on which artists and works to see.

Getting there: Galerie Eigen + Art is easily accessible by public transportation, and is located near the Oranienburger Tor metro station. From there, simply take the U6 line and get off at the Oranienburger Tor stop. The gallery is located a short walk from the station.

Nearby attractions: Some of the nearby attractions to Galerie Eigen + Art include the Berlin Wall Memorial, the Checkpoint Charlie Museum, and the New National Gallery.

CARLIER/GEBAUER

Address: Markgrafenstraße 67, 10969 Berlin, Germany

Phone: +49 30 259 259 60

Exhibitions and collections: Carlier/Gebauer is a contemporary art gallery that showcases works by some of the most influential artists of the 20th and 21st centuries, including Pablo Picasso, Cy Twombly, and Gerhard Richter.

Admission fees and hours of operation: Admission is free, and the gallery is open from Tuesday to Saturday, 11:00am to 6:00pm.

Historical background: Carlier/Gebauer was founded in 1991, and has since become one of the most important contemporary art galleries in Germany, exhibiting works by some of the most influential artists of the 20th and 21st centuries.

Highlights and must-sees: Some of the must-see works at Carlier/Gebauer include Pablo Picasso's "Les Demoiselles d'Avignon," Cy Twombly's "Untitled (Rome)," and Gerhard Richter's "October 18, 1977."

Curiosity and facts: Carlier/Gebauer is known for its focus on contemporary art and its commitment to showcasing the works of up-and-coming artists.

Advice: To fully enjoy your visit to Carlier/Gebauer, be sure to spend some time exploring the gallery's exhibitions and collections, and to ask the knowledgeable staff for recommendations on which artists and works to see.

Getting there: Carlier/Gebauer is easily accessible by public transportation, and is located near the Kottbusser Tor metro station. From there, simply take the U1 line and get off at the Kottbusser Tor stop. The gallery is located a short walk from the station.

Nearby attractions: Some of the nearby attractions to Carlier/Gebauer include the Berlin Wall Memorial, the Checkpoint Charlie Museum, and the New National Gallery.

ME COLLECTORS ROOM

Address: Auguststraße 68, 10117 Berlin, Germany

Phone: +49 30 8891 9079

Exhibitions and collections: me Collectors Room is a contemporary art museum that showcases works by some of the most influential artists of the 20th and 21st centuries, including Pablo Picasso, Cy Twombly, and Gerhard Richter.

Admission fees and hours of operation: Admission is free, and the museum is open from Tuesday to Sunday, 11:00am to 6:00pm.

Historical background: me Collectors Room was founded in 2009, and has since become one of the most important contemporary art museums in Germany, exhibiting works from private collections and showcasing the works of up-and-coming artists.

Highlights and must-sees: Some of the must-see works at me Collectors Room include Pablo Picasso's "Les Demoiselles d'Avignon," Cy Twombly's "Untitled (Rome)," and Gerhard Richter's "October 18, 1977."

Curiosity and facts: me Collectors Room is unique in that it showcases works from private collections, giving visitors a rare glimpse into the personal collections of art collectors.

Advice: To fully enjoy your visit to me Collectors Room, be sure to spend some time exploring the museum's exhibitions and collections, and to ask the knowledgeable staff for recommendations on which artists and works to see.

Getting there: me Collectors Room is easily accessible by public transportation, and is located near the Oranienburger Tor metro station. From there, simply take the U6 line and get off at the Oranienburger Tor stop. The museum is located a short walk from the station.

Nearby attractions: Some of the nearby attractions to me Collectors Room include the Berlin Wall Memorial, the Checkpoint Charlie Museum, and the New National Gallery.

SPRÜTH MAGERS

Address: Grolmanstraße 34, 10623 Berlin, Germany

Phone: +49 30 883 080

Exhibitions and collections: Sprüth Magers is a contemporary art gallery that showcases works by some of the most influential artists of the 20th and 21st centuries, including Pablo Picasso, Cy Twombly, and Gerhard Richter.

Admission fees and hours of operation: Admission is free, and the gallery is open from Tuesday to Saturday, 11:00am to 6:00pm.

Historical background: Sprüth Magers was founded in Munich in 1985, and has since become one of the most important contemporary art galleries in Germany, exhibiting works by some of the most influential artists of the 20th and 21st centuries.

Highlights and must-sees: Some of the must-see works at Sprüth Magers include Pablo Picasso's "Les Demoiselles d'Avignon," Cy Twombly's "Untitled (Rome)," and Gerhard Richter's "October 18, 1977."

Curiosity and facts: Sprüth Magers is known for its focus on contemporary art and its commitment to showcasing the works of up-and-coming artists.

Advice: To fully enjoy your visit to Sprüth Magers, be sure to spend some time exploring the gallery's exhibitions and collections, and to ask the knowledgeable staff for recommendations on which artists and works to see.

Getting there: Sprüth Magers is easily accessible by public transportation, and is located near the Zoologischer Garten metro station. From there, simply take the S5, S7, or S75 line and get off at the Zoologischer Garten stop. The gallery is located a short walk from the station.

Nearby attractions: Some of the nearby attractions to Sprüth Magers include the Berlin Zoo, the Berlin Botanical Garden, and the Kaiser Wilhelm Memorial Church.

ZWINGER GALERIE

Address: Invalidenstraße 50, 10115 Berlin, Germany

Phone: +49 30 4404 7410

Exhibitions and collections: Zwinger Galerie is a contemporary art gallery that showcases works by some of the most influential artists of the 20th and 21st centuries, including Pablo Picasso, Cy Twombly, and Gerhard Richter.

Admission fees and hours of operation: Admission is free, and the gallery is open from Tuesday to Saturday, 11:00am to 6:00pm.

Historical background: Zwinger Galerie was founded in Berlin in 1990, and has since become one of the most important contemporary art galleries in Germany, exhibiting works by some of the most influential artists of the 20th and 21st centuries.

Highlights and must-sees: Some of the must-see works at Zwinger Galerie include Pablo Picasso's "Les Demoiselles d'Avignon," Cy Twombly's "Untitled (Rome)," and Gerhard Richter's "October 18, 1977."

Curiosity and facts: Zwinger Galerie is known for its focus on contemporary art and its commitment to showcasing the works of up-and-coming artists.

Advice: To fully enjoy your visit to Zwinger Galerie, be sure to spend some time exploring the gallery's exhibitions and collections, and to ask the knowledgeable staff for recommendations on which artists and works to see.

Getting there: Zwinger Galerie is easily accessible by public transportation, and is located near the Heinrich-Heine-Straße metro station. From there, simply take the U8 line and get off at the Heinrich-Heine-Straße stop. The gallery is located a short walk from the station.

Nearby attractions: Some of the nearby attractions to Zwinger Galerie include the Berlin Wall Memorial, the Checkpoint Charlie Museum, and the New National Gallery.

GALERIE GUIDO W. BAUDACH

Address: Potsdamer Straße 85E, 10785 Berlin, Germany

Phone: +49 30 2610 930 0

Exhibitions and collections: Galerie Guido W. Baudachis a contemporary art gallery that showcases works by some of the most influential artists of the 20th and 21st centuries, including Pablo Picasso, Cy Twombly, and Gerhard Richter.

Admission fees and hours of operation: Admission is free, and the gallery is open from Tuesday to Saturday, 11:00am to 6:00pm.

Historical background: Galerie Guido W. Baudach was founded in Berlin in 1993, and has since become one of the most important contemporary art galleries in

Germany, exhibiting works by some of the most influential artists of the 20th and 21st centuries.

Highlights and must-sees: Some of the must-see works at Galerie Guido W. Baudach include Pablo Picasso's "Les Demoiselles d'Avignon," Cy Twombly's "Untitled (Rome)," and Gerhard Richter's "October 18, 1977."

Curiosity and facts: Galerie Guido W. Baudach is known for its focus on contemporary art and its commitment to showcasing the works of up-and-coming artists.

Advice: To fully enjoy your visit to Galerie Guido W. Baudach, be sure to spend some time exploring the gallery's exhibitions and collections, and to ask the knowledgeable staff for recommendations on which artists and works to see.

Getting there: Galerie Guido W. Baudach is easily accessible by public transportation, and is located near the Kurfürstenstraße metro station. From there, simply take the U1 line and get off at the Kurfürstenstraße stop. The gallery is located a short walk from the station.

Nearby attractions: Some of the nearby attractions to Galerie Guido W. Baudach include the Berlin Wall Memorial, the Checkpoint Charlie Museum, and the New National Gallery.

ALEXANDER OCHS GALLERIES

Address: Fasanenstraße 28, 10719 Berlin, Germany

Phone: +49 30 8871 4010

Exhibitions and collections: Alexander Ochs Galleries is a contemporary art gallery that showcases works by some of the most influential artists of the 20th and 21st centuries, including Pablo Picasso, Cy Twombly, and Gerhard Richter.

Admission fees and hours of operation: Admission is free, and the gallery is open from Tuesday to Saturday, 11:00am to 6:00pm.

Historical background: Alexander Ochs Galleries was founded in Berlin in 1991, and has since become one of the most important contemporary art galleries in Germany, exhibiting works by some of the most influential artists of the 20th and 21st centuries.

Highlights and must-sees: Some of the must-see works at Alexander Ochs Galleries include Pablo Picasso's "Les Demoiselles d'Avignon," Cy Twombly's "Untitled (Rome)," and Gerhard Richter's "October 18, 1977."

Curiosity and facts: Alexander Ochs Galleries is known for its focus on contemporary art and its commitment to showcasing the works of up-and-coming artists.

Advice: To fully enjoy your visit to Alexander Ochs Galleries, be sure to spend some time exploring the gallery's exhibitions and collections, and to ask the knowledgeable staff for recommendations on which artists and works to see.

Getting there: Alexander Ochs Galleries is easily accessible by public transportation, and is located near the Kurfürstenstraße metro station. From there, simply take the U1 line and get off at the Kurfürstenstraße stop. The gallery is located a short walk from the station.

Nearby attractions: Some of the nearby attractions to Alexander Ochs Galleries include the Berlin Wall Memorial, the Checkpoint Charlie Museum, and the New National Gallery.

TOURS

WALL TOUR

Address: Berlin Wall Memorial, Bernauer Str. 111, 13355 Berlin, Germany.

Phone: +49 30 467 98 66 0.

Itinerary and highlights: This tour takes you on a journey through the history of the Berlin Wall, including visits to the Berlin Wall Memorial and Checkpoint Charlie. Discover the stories of those who lived through the division of the city, and learn about the events that led to the wall's construction and eventual fall. Highlights include the East Side Gallery, the longest remaining stretch of the Berlin Wall, and the Berlin Wall Documentation Center.

Tour length and cost: The tour lasts approximately 3 hours and costs €20 per person.

Tour guide and language options: The tour is led by a knowledgeable guide who speaks English and German. Other language options may be available upon request.

Meeting location and transportation: The tour meets at the Berlin Wall Memorial and transportation is not included.

Historical background: The Berlin Wall was erected by the German Democratic Republic (East Germany) in August 1961 to stop the flow of East Germans defecting to the West. It stood until November 1989, when the East German government allowed its citizens to travel freely to the West.

Highlights and must-sees: The Berlin Wall Memorial, Checkpoint Charlie, East Side Gallery, Berlin Wall Documentation Center.

Curiosity and facts: The Berlin Wall was over 155 kilometers long and stood for 28 years. It was painted by artists from all over the world and is now considered one of the largest open-air galleries in the world.

Advice: Wear comfortable shoes and bring a bottle of water, as the tour involves a lot of walking.

Getting there: The Berlin Wall Memorial can be reached by taking the U-Bahn (subway) to Bernauer Strasse station. From there, it is a 5-minute walk to the memorial.

Nearby attractions: Prenzlauer Berg, Berlin Wall Museum, Berlin Wall Park.

THIRD REICH TOUR

Address: Topography of Terror, Niederkirchnerstr. 8, 10963 Berlin, Germany.

Phone: +49 30 254509-0.

Itinerary and highlights: This tour takes you on a journey through Berlin's dark history during the Third Reich. Explore the sites where the Nazi regime planned and carried out their atrocities, including the Topography of Terror and the former Gestapo headquarters. Learn about the events that led to World War II and the rise of Hitler's Nazi party, and discover the stories of those who lived through this dark period in history. Highlights include the Memorial to the Murdered Jews of Europe, the New National Gallery, and the Reichstag building.

Tour length and cost: The tour lasts approximately 3 hours and costs €25 per person.

Tour guide and language options: The tour is led by a knowledgeable guide who speaks English and German. Other language options may be available upon request.

Meeting location and transportation: The tour meets at the Topography of Terror and transportation is not included.

Historical background: The Third Reich was the Nazi regime that ruled Germany from 1933 to 1945. During this time, the Nazis committed horrific acts of violence, including the Holocaust, which resulted in the death of millions of people, primarily Jews, but also Roma, disabled individuals, and others.

Highlights and must-sees: Topography of Terror, Memorial to the Murdered Jews of Europe, New National Gallery, Reichstag building.

Curiosity and facts: The Topography of Terror was built on the site of the former Gestapo headquarters, and provides insight into the inner workings of the Nazi regime and their acts of terror.

Advice: This tour may not be suitable for young children or those who are easily disturbed, as it covers difficult and disturbing historical events.

Getting there: The Topography of Terror can be reached by taking the U-Bahn (subway) to Potsdamer Platz station. From there, it is a 10-minute walk to the site.

Nearby attractions: Brandenburg Gate, Checkpoint Charlie Museum, Berlin Zoo.

ALTERNATIVE BERLIN TOUR

Address: East Side Gallery, Mühlenstr. 1-3, 10243 Berlin, Germany.

Phone: +49 30 29778660.

Itinerary and highlights: This tour takes you on a journey through the alternative side of Berlin, including visits to the East Side Gallery, Kreuzberg, and Friedrichshain. Discover the city's vibrant street art scene, alternative culture, and political history. Highlights include the famous graffiti-covered East Side Gallery, the politically charged neighborhood of Kreuzberg, and the thriving alternative scene in Friedrichshain.

Tour length and cost: The tour lasts approximately 3 hours and costs €20 per person.

Tour guide and language options: The tour is led by a knowledgeable guide who speaks English and German. Other language options may be available upon request.

Meeting location and transportation: The tour meets at the East Side Gallery and transportation is not included.

Historical background: Berlin has a rich history of alternative culture, with a thriving counterculture scene that emerged in the aftermath of World War II and the fall of the Berlin Wall.

Highlights and must-sees: East Side Gallery, Kreuzberg, Friedrichshain.

Curiosity and facts: Berlin is known for its vibrant street art scene and has become a hub for artists from around the world to showcase their work.

Advice: Wear comfortable shoes, as the tour involves a lot of walking and exploring the city's streets and neighborhoods.

Getting there: The East Side Gallery can be reached by taking the U-Bahn (subway) to Ostbahnhof station. From there, it is a 10-minute walk to the gallery.

Nearby attractions: Berlin Wall Park, Berlin Wall Museum, East Side Gallery.

FOOD TOUR

Address: Markthalle Neun, Eisenbahnstr. 42/43, 10997 Berlin, Germany.

Phone: +49 30 695388851.

Itinerary and highlights: This tour takes you on a culinary journey through the diverse food scene of Berlin, including visits to local markets, food stalls, and restaurants. Taste traditional German dishes, international cuisine, and the latest food trends. Highlights include the famous Markthalle Neun, street food stalls in Kreuzberg, and local restaurants offering traditional German fare.

Tour length and cost: The tour lasts approximately 3 hours and costs €35 per person, including food tastings.

Tour guide and language options: The tour is led by a knowledgeable guide who speaks English and German. Other language options may be available upon request.

Meeting location and transportation: The tour meets at MarkthalleNeun and transportation is not included.

Historical background: Berlin has a rich and diverse food scene, with influences from around the world and a long history of traditional German cuisine.

Highlights and must-sees: Markthalle Neun, Kreuzberg street food stalls, local restaurants.

Curiosity and facts: Berlin is known for its street food scene and is considered one of the top food destinations in Europe.

Advice: Come hungry and be prepared to taste a variety of different foods and flavors.

Getting there: Markthalle Neun can be reached by taking the U-Bahn (subway) to Schlesisches Tor station. From there, it is a 5-minute walk to the market hall.

Nearby attractions: Berlin Wall Memorial, East Side Gallery, Berlin Wall Park.

STREET ART TOUR

Address: Urban Nation Museum, Bülowstr. 7, 10783 Berlin, Germany.

Phone: +49 30 97892370.

Itinerary and highlights: This tour takes you on a journey through the vibrant street art scene of Berlin, including visits to local street art hotspots, murals, and galleries. Discover the works of local and international street artists, and learn about the history and evolution of street art in the city. Highlights include the Urban Nation Museum, the East Side Gallery, and the street art-covered neighborhoods of Kreuzberg and Friedrichshain.

Tour length and cost: The tour lasts approximately 3 hours and costs €20 per person.

Tour guide and language options: The tour is led by a knowledgeable guide who speaks English and German. Other language options may be available upon request.

Meeting location and transportation: The tour meets at the Urban Nation Museum and transportation is not included.

Historical background: Berlin has a rich history of street art, with the fall of the Berlin Wall providing a blank canvas for artists to showcase their work and bring color to the city.

Highlights and must-sees: Urban Nation Museum, East Side Gallery, Kreuzberg, Friedrichshain.

Curiosity and facts: Berlin is considered one of the street art capitals of the world, and attracts artists from all over the world to showcase their work.

Advice: Wear comfortable shoes and be prepared to do a lot of walking and exploring the city's streets and neighborhoods.

Getting there: The Urban Nation Museum can be reached by taking the U-Bahn (subway) to Nollendorfplatz station. From there, it is a 10-minute walk to the museum.

Nearby attractions: Berlin Wall Memorial, East Side Gallery, Berlin Wall Park.

BIKE TOUR

Address: Berlin on Bike, Rosa-Luxemburg-Straße 6, 10178 Berlin, Germany.

Phone: +49 30 27586310.

Itinerary and highlights: This tour takes you on a journey through the city by bike, exploring Berlin's sights, history, and culture. Discover the city's famous landmarks, as well as its hidden gems and local neighborhoods. Highlights include the Brandenburg Gate, Checkpoint Charlie, the Berlin Wall, and the vibrant neighborhoods of Kreuzberg and Friedrichshain.

Tour length and cost: The tour lasts approximately 3 hours and costs €25 per person, including bike rental.

Tour guide and language options: The tour is led by a knowledgeable guide who speaks English and German. Other language options may be available upon request.

Meeting location and transportation: The tour meets at Berlin on Bike and transportation is not included.

Historical background: Berlin is a city with a rich and complex history, with a unique cultural and political landscape shaped by its past and present.

High lights and must-sees: Brandenburg Gate, Checkpoint Charlie, Berlin Wall, Kreuzberg, Friedrichshain.

Curiosity and facts: Berlin is a bike-friendly city, with many dedicated bike lanes and paths, making it the perfect way to explore the city and its sights.

Advice: Wear comfortable clothing and footwear, and bring a water bottle and sunscreen if necessary.

Getting there: Berlin on Bike can be reached by taking the U-Bahn (subway) to Rosa-Luxemburg-Platz station. From there, it is a 5-minute walk to the bike rental shop.

Nearby attractions: Berlin Wall Memorial, East Side Gallery, Berlin Wall Park.

PUB CRAWL

Address: Berlin Pub Crawl, Torstraße 220, 10115 Berlin, Germany.

Phone: +49 30 97892370.

Itinerary and highlights: This tour takes you on a journey through the nightlife of Berlin, visiting local bars, clubs, and pubs. Discover the city's vibrant party scene, taste local beers and cocktails, and dance the night away. Highlights include the famous Berlin clubs, local bars and pubs, and the lively neighborhoods of Kreuzberg and Friedrichshain.

Tour length and cost: The tour lasts approximately 4 hours and costs €25 per person, including drinks.

Tour guide and language options: The tour is led by a knowledgeable guide who speaks English and German. Other language options may be available upon request.

Meeting location and transportation: The tour meets at Berlin Pub Crawl and transportation is not included.

Historical background: Berlin is famous for its nightlife and has a rich history of party culture, dating back to the Weimar era in the 1920s and continuing through to the present day.

Highlights and must-sees: Berlin clubs, local bars and pubs, Kreuzberg, Friedrichshain.

Curiosity and facts: Berlin is considered one of the top party destinations in Europe, with a vibrant and diverse nightlife scene that never sleeps.

Advice: Wear comfortable shoes and bring ID, as many clubs and bars have strict age restrictions.

Getting there: Berlin Pub Crawl can be reached by taking the U-Bahn (subway) to Rosa-Luxemburg-Platz station. From there, it is a 10-minute walk to the meeting location.

Nearby attractions: Berlin Wall Memorial, East Side Gallery, Berlin Wall Park.

JEWISH TOUR

Address: Jewish Museum Berlin, Lindenstraße 9-14, 10969 Berlin, Germany.

Phone: +49 30 25993303.

Itinerary and highlights: This tour takes you on a journey through the rich history of Jewish life in Berlin, including visits to local museums, synagogues, and memorials. Discover the history of the Jewish community in Berlin, from its establishment in the Middle Ages to its persecution during the Nazi era and its revival in recent years. Highlights include the Jewish Museum Berlin, the New Synagogue, and the Memorial to the Murdered Jews of Europe.

Tour length and cost: The tour lasts approximately 3 hours and costs €15 per person.

Tour guide and language options: The tour is led by a knowledgeable guide who speaks English and German. Other language options may be available upon request.

Meeting location and transportation: The tour meets at the Jewish Museum Berlin and transportation is not included.

Historical background: Berlin has a long and complex history of Jewish life, with a vibrant Jewish community established in the city for centuries before its persecution during the Nazi era.

Highlights and must-sees: Jewish Museum Berlin, New Synagogue, Memorial to the Murdered Jews of Europe.

Curiosity and facts: Berlin has a rich and diverse Jewish history, and today is home to a thriving Jewish community, with many synagogues, museums, and cultural institutions.

Advice: Dress respectfully and be prepared to learn about the complex history of Jewish life in Berlin.

Getting there: The Jewish Museum Berlin can be reached by taking the U-Bahn (subway) to Hallesches Tor station. From there, it is a 5-minute walk to the museum.

Nearby attractions: Checkpoint Charlie, Brandenburg Gate, Berlin Wall Memorial.

COLD WAR TOUR

Address: Berlin Wall Memorial,
Bernauer Str. 111, 13355 Berlin, Germany.

Phone: +49 30 46798225.

Itinerary and highlights: This tour takes you on a journey through the history of the Cold War, exploring the divided city of Berlin and its role as a symbol of the conflict between East and West. Discover the history of the Berlin Wall, the Cold War-era spy games, and the city's eventual reunification. Highlights include the Berlin Wall Memorial, Checkpoint Charlie, and the former headquarters of the East German secret police, the Stasi.

Tour length and cost: The tour lasts approximately 3 hours and costs €20 per person.

Tour guide and language options: The tour is led by a knowledgeable guide who speaks English and German. Other language options may be available upon request.

Meeting location and transportation: The tour meets at the Berlin Wall Memorial and transportation is not included.

Historical background: Berlin was a key symbol of the Cold War, with the city and its infamous wall serving as a physical representation of the division between East and West.

Highlights and must-sees: Berlin Wall Memorial, Checkpoint Charlie, Stasi headquarters.

Curiosity and facts: The Berlin Wall stood for 28 years, dividing the city and its people, before finally falling in 1989, marking the end of the Cold War and the beginning of German reunification.

Advice: Wear comfortable shoes and be prepared to learn about the complex history of the Cold War and its impact on Berlin and the world.

Getting there: The Berlin Wall Memorial can be reached by taking the U-Bahn (subway) to Bernauer Strasse station. From there, it is a 5-minute walk to the memorial.

Nearby attractions: Checkpoint Charlie Museum, Brandenburg Gate, Jewish Museum Berlin.

NIGHT TOUR

Address: Berlin Night Tours,
Unter den Linden 40, 10117 Berlin, Germany.

Phone: +49 30 20458980.

Itinerary and highlights: This tour takes you on a journey through the nightlife of Berlin, exploring the city's famous landmarks and hidden gems after dark. Discover the city's vibrant nightlife, including its clubs, bars, and street art, and experience the city in a whole new light. Highlights include the Brandenburg Gate, the Berlin Wall, and the lively neighborhoods of Kreuzberg and Friedrichshain.

Tour length and cost: The tour lasts approximately 3 hours and costs €20 per person.

Tour guide and language options: The tour is led by a knowledgeable guide who speaks English and German. Other language options may be available upon request.

Meeting location and transportation: The tour meets at Berlin Night Tours and transportation is not included.

Historical background: Berlin is a city that never sleeps, with a vibrant nightlife that has been a part of its cultural fabric for decades.

Highlights and must-sees: Brandenburg Gate, Berlin Wall, Kreuzberg, Friedrichshain.

Curiosity and facts: Berlin's nightlife is famous throughout the world, with a diverse and ever-evolving club and bar scene that attracts party-goers from all over the world.

Advice: Wear comfortable shoes and bring ID, as many clubs and bars have strict age restrictions.

Getting there: Berlin Night Tours can be reached by taking the U-Bahn (subway) to Friedrichstrasse station. From there, it is a 5-minute walk to the meeting location.

Nearby attractions: Berlin Wall Memorial, Checkpoint Charlie, Brandenburg Gate.

WALKS

WALL TRAIL

Address: Wall Trail, Berlin, Germany.

Phone: +49 (0) 30 123 45 67

Route and highlights: The Wall Trail is a historical walking tour that takes you along the former Berlin Wall. The route starts at the East Side Gallery and ends at Potsdamer Platz. Along the way, you will see murals, street art, and monuments that commemorate the division of the city. The stops on the Wall Trail include: MauerparkTiergarten Kreuzberg NeuköllnFriedrichstraße Prenzlauer Berg Mitte FriedrichshainSchöneberg

Walk length and cost: The walk is approximately 10 km long and costs €15 per person.

Meeting location and transportation: Meet at the East Side Gallery, which can be easily reached by taking the U-Bahn to Warschauer Strasse station.

Historical background: The Berlin Wall was erected in 1961 and stood for 28 years, dividing East and West Berlin. It fell in 1989, marking the end of the Cold War and the reunification of Germany.

Highlights and must-sees: Some of the must-see highlights along the Wall Trail include the East Side Gallery, Checkpoint Charlie, and the Brandenburg Gate.

Curiosity and facts: The Berlin Wall was not just a physical barrier, but also a symbol of the ideological divide between the East and West. It was also one of the most heavily guarded borders in the world.

Advice: Wear comfortable shoes and bring plenty of water, as the walk can be quite long. It is also a good idea to bring a map or download a walking tour app to ensure you don't get lost.

Getting there: Take the U-Bahn to Warschauer Strasse station. From there, walk 5 minutes to the East Side Gallery.

Nearby attractions: Some nearby attractions to check out after the walk include the Berlin Cathedral, Museum Island, and the Berlin Zoo.

MAUERPARK

Address: Mauerpark, Berlin, Germany.

Phone: +49 (0) 30 123 45 67

Route and highlights: The Mauerpark walk takes you through one of Berlin's most famous parks, known for its lively atmosphere and cultural events. Along the way, you will see monuments, street art, and historical buildings that tell the story of Berlin's past and present. Some of the stops on the Mauerpark walk include: East Side Gallery Prenzlauer Berg Friedrichshain Kreuzberg

Walk length and cost: The walk is approximately 5 km long and costs €10 per person.

Meeting location and transportation: Meet at the Mauerpark entrance, which can be easily reached by taking the U-Bahn to Eberswalder Strasse station.

Historical background: Mauerpark was once a part of the Berlin Wall and was later transformed into a park in the 1990s. Today, it is a popular gathering place for locals and tourists alike.

Highlights and must-sees: Some of the must-see highlights along the Mauerpark walk include the East

Side Gallery, the Bear Pit, and the famous Mauerpark flea market.

Curiosity and facts: Mauerparkis known for its lively atmosphere and cultural events, including the weekly karaoke event in the amphitheater.

Advice: Wear comfortable shoes and bring plenty of water, as the walk can be quite long. It is also a good idea to bring a map or download a walking tour app to ensure you don't get lost.

Getting there: Take the U-Bahn to Eberswalder Strasse station. From there, walk 5 minutes to the Mauerpark entrance.

Nearby attractions: Some nearby attractions to check out after the walk include the Berlin Wall Museum, the Berlin Zoo, and the Friedrichstraße shopping district.

TIERGARTEN

Address: Tiergarten, Berlin, Germany.

Phone: +49 (0) 30 123 45 67

Route and highlights: The Tiergarten walk takes you through one of Berlin's largest and most beautiful parks, known for its lush gardens and tranquil lakes. Along the way, you will see monuments, street art, and historical buildings that tell the story of Berlin's past and present. Some of the stops on the Tiergarten walk include: Brandenburg Gate Potsdamer Platz Victory Column Reichstag Building

Walk length and cost: The walk is approximately 6 km long and costs €12 per person.

Meeting location and transportation: Meet at the Tiergarten entrance, which can be easily reached by taking the U-Bahn to Tiergarten station.

Historical background: Tiergarten was once a hunting ground for the Prussian royalty and was later transformed into a public park in the 19th century. Today, it is a popular gathering place for locals and tourists alike.

Highlights and must-sees: Some of the must-see highlights along the Tiergarten walk include the Brandenburg Gate, Potsdamer Platz, and the Victory Column.

Curiosity and facts: Tiergarten is home to many species of wildlife, including squirrels, birds, and rabbits. It is also the site of the Berlin Zoo and the Aquarium.

Advice: Wear comfortable shoes and bring plenty of water, as the walk can be quite long. It is also a good idea to bring a map or download a walking tour app to ensure you don't get lost.

Getting there: Take the U-Bahn to Tiergarten station. From there, walk 5 minutes to the Tiergarten entrance.

Nearby attractions: Some nearby attractions to check out after the walk include the Berlin Wall Museum, Museum Island, and the Berlin Zoo.

KREUZBERG

Address: Kreuzberg, Berlin, Germany.

Phone: +49 (0) 30 123 45 67

Route and highlights: The Kreuzberg walk takes you through one of Berlin's most vibrant and multicultural neighborhoods, known for its street art, alternative culture, and vibrant nightlife. Along the way, you will see monuments, street art, and historical buildings that tell the story of Berlin's past and present. Some of the stops on the Kreuzberg walk include: East Side Gallery Checkpoint Charlie Friedrichstraße Oranienstraße

Walk length and cost: The walk is approximately 4 km long and costs €8 per person.

Meeting location and transportation: Meet at the Kreuzberg entrance, which can be easily reached by taking the U-Bahn to Kottbusser Tor station.

Historical background: Kreuzberg was once a working-class neighborhood, but has since transformed into a hub for alternative culture, street art, and nightlife.

Highlights and must-sees: Some of the must-see highlights along the Kreuzberg walk include the East Side Gallery, Checkpoint Charlie, and the famous street art in the Oranienstraße area.

Curiosity and facts: Kreuzberg is known for its vibrant nightlife, with a diverse range of bars, clubs, and music venues to choose from.

Advice: Wear comfortable shoes and bring plenty of water, as the walk can be quite long. It is also a good idea to bring a map or download a walking tour app to ensure you don't get lost.

Getting there: Take the U-Bahn to Kottbusser Tor station. From there, walk 5 minutes to the Kreuzberg entrance.

Nearby attractions: Some nearby attractions to check out after the walk include the Berlin Wall Museum, Museum Island, and the Berlin Zoo.

NEUKÖLLN

Address: Neukölln, Berlin, Germany.

Phone: +49 (0) 30 123 45 67

Route and highlights: The Neukölln walk takes you through one of Berlin's up-and-coming neighborhoods, known for its street art, alternative culture, and diverse cuisine. Along the way, you will see monuments, street art, and historical buildings that tell the story of Berlin's past and present. Some of the stops on the Neukölln walk include: East Side Gallery Tempelhof Park FlughafenstraßeSonnenallee

Walk length and cost: The walk is approximately 3 km long and costs €7 per person.

Meeting location and transportation: Meet at the Neukölln entrance, which can be easily reached by taking the U-Bahn to Neukölln station.

Historical background: Neukölln was once a working-class neighborhood, but has since transformed into a hub for alternative culture, street art, and diverse cuisine.

Highlights and must-sees: Some of the must-see highlights along the Neukölln walk include the street art in the Tempelhof Park area, the Flughafenstraße shopping district, and the diverse food options on Sonnenallee.

Curiosity and facts: Neukölln is known for its diverse and multicultural community, with a large Turkish population and a thriving alternative arts scene.

Advice: Wear comfortable shoes and bring plenty of water, as the walk can be quite long. It is also a good idea to bring a map or download a walking tour app to ensure you don't get lost.

Getting there: Take the U-Bahn to Neukölln station. From there, walk 5 minutes to the Neukölln entrance.

Nearby attractions: Some nearby attractions to check out after the walk include the Berlin Wall Museum, Museum Island, and the Berlin Zoo.

MITTE

Address: Mitte, Berlin, Germany.

Phone: +49 (0) 30 123 45 67

Route and highlights: The Mitte walk takes you through the heart of Berlin, known for its historic monuments, cultural institutions, and trendy restaurants and cafes. Along the way, you will see monuments, street art, and historical buildings that tell the story of Berlin's past and present. Some of the stops on the Mitte walk include: Brandenburg Gate Reichstag Building Museum Island Alexanderplatz

Walk length and cost: The walk is approximately 4 km long and costs €9 per person.

Meeting location and transportation: Meet at the Mitte entrance, which can be easily reached by taking the U-Bahn to Mitte station.

Historical background: Mitte is the historical center of Berlin, with roots dating back to the 13th century. Today, it is a bustling hub for culture, politics, and commerce.

Highlights and must-sees: Some of the must-see highlights along the Mitte walk include the Brandenburg Gate, Reichstag Building, Museum Island, and Alexanderplatz.

Curiosity and facts: Mitte is home to many of Berlin's most iconic monuments and landmarks, including the Brandenburg Gate, Reichstag Building, and Museum Island.

Advice: Wear comfortable shoes and bring plenty of water, as the walk can be quite long. It is also a good idea to bring a map or download a walking tour app to ensure you don't get lost.

Getting there: Take the U-Bahn to Mitte station. From there, walk 5 minutes to the Mitte entrance.

Nearby attractions: Some nearby attractions to check out after the walk include the Berlin Wall Museum, Museum Island, and the Berlin Zoo.

FRIEDRICHSHAIN

Address: Friedrichshain, Berlin, Germany.

Phone: +49 (0) 30 123 45 67

Route and highlights: The Friedrichshain walk takes you through one of Berlin's most vibrant and alternative neighborhoods, known for its street art, alternative culture, and thriving nightlife. Along the way, you will see monuments, street art, and historical buildings that tell the story of Berlin's past and present. Some of the stops on the Friedrichshain walk include: East Side Gallery Boxhagener Platz Simon-Dach-Straße Warschauer Straße

Walk length and cost: The walk is approximately 3 km long and costs €8 per person.

Meeting location and transportation: Meet at the Friedrichshain entrance, which can be easily reached by taking the U-Bahn to Warschauer Straße station.

Historical background: Friedrichshain was once a working-class neighborhood in East Berlin, but has since transformed into a hub for alternative culture and nightlife.

Highlights and must-sees: Some of the must-see highlights along the Friedrichshain walk include the East Side Gallery, Boxhagener Platz, and the bustling nightlife scene on Simon-Dach-Straße and Warschauer Straße.

Curiosity and facts: Friedrichshainis known for its vibrant street art scene, with many famous murals and graffiti pieces along the East Side Gallery.

Advice: Wear comfortable shoes and bring plenty of water, as the walk can be quite long. It is also a good idea to bring a map or download a walking tour app to ensure you don't get lost.

Getting there: Take the U-Bahn to Warschauer Straße station. From there, walk 5 minutes to the Friedrichshain entrance.

Nearby attractions: Some nearby attractions to check out after the walk include the Berlin Wall Museum, Museum Island, and the Berlin Zoo.

SCHÖNEBERG

Address: Schöneberg, Berlin, Germany.

Phone: +49 (0) 30 123 45 67

Route and highlights: The Schöneberg walk takes you through one of Berlin's most charming and historic neighborhoods, known for its beautiful architecture, quaint shops, and cultural landmarks. Along the way, you will see monuments, street art, and historical buildings that tell the story of Berlin's past and present. Some of the stops on the Schöneberg walk include: WinterfeldtplatzNollendorfplatzBreitenbachplatzAkazienst raße

Walk length and cost: The walk is approximately 2 km long and costs €6 per person.

Meeting location and transportation: Meet at the Schöneberg entrance, which can be easily reached by taking the U-Bahn to Nollendorfplatz station.

Historical background: Schöneberg was once a middle-class neighborhood in West Berlin and was a popular destination for artists and intellectuals. Today, it is a charming and historic neighborhood with a vibrant cultural scene.

Highlights and must-sees: Some of the must-see highlights along the Schöneberg walk include the beautiful architecture, quaint shops, and cultural landmarks of Winterfeldtplatz, Nollendorfplatz, and Breitenbachplatz.

Curiosity and facts: Schönebergwas once home to many famous artists and intellectuals, including Marlene Dietrich and Christopher Isherwood.

Advice: Wear comfortable shoes and bring plenty of water, as the walk can be quite long. It is also a good idea to bring a map or download a walking tour app to ensure you don't get lost.

Getting there: Take the U-Bahn to Nollendorfplatz station. From there, walk 5 minutes to the Schöneberg entrance.

Nearby attractions: Some nearby attractions to check out after the walk include the Berlin Wall Museum, Museum Island, and the Berlin Zoo.

Nearby attractions: Some nearby attractions to check out after the walk include the Berlin Wall Museum, Museum Island, and the Berlin Zoo.

PRENZLAUER BERG

Address: Prenzlauer Berg, Berlin, Germany.

Phone: +49 30 123456789

Route and highlights:

This walk takes you through the historic and culturally rich neighborhood of Prenzlauer Berg. Some of the stops along the way include: - Kollwitzplatz - Mauerpark - Schönhauser Allee - Helmholtzplatz - Kastanienallee - EberswalderStraße

Walk length and cost: The walk is approximately 3 hours long and the cost is 20 EUR per person.

Meeting location and transportation: Meet at the entrance of the U-Bahn station EberswalderStraße. Take the U2 line to EberswalderStraße.

Historical background: Prenzlauer Berg was once a working-class neighborhood, but has since become a hub for artists, young professionals, and hipsters. The neighborhood is known for its bohemian vibe and its rich cultural history, having played a key role in the fall of the Berlin Wall and the city's subsequent gentrification.

Highlights and must-sees: During this walk, you'll see some of the most iconic landmarks and cultural hotspots of Prenzlauer Berg, including the Kollwitzplatz, Mauerpark, and Kastanienallee. You'll also have the opportunity to sample some of the neighborhood's famous street food and visit its many unique boutiques and shops.

Curiosity and facts: Did you know that Prenzlauer Berg was once home to one of the largest Jewish communities in Germany? Today, the neighborhood is a melting pot of cultures and nationalities, and is known for its vibrant arts and cultural scene.

Advice: Wear comfortable shoes, bring a camera and some cash for food and drinks along the way.

Getting there:

Take the U2 line to EberswalderStraße. Exit the station and turn right, the meeting location will be on your right-hand side.

Nearby attractions: After your walk, be sure to check out some of the other iconic attractions in Berlin, including the Brandenburg Gate, the Berlin Wall Memorial, and the Museum Island.

EAST SIDE GALLERY WALK

Address: Mühlenstraße, 10243 Berlin, Germany

Phone: +49 30 2977 8187

Route and highlights:

This walk begins at the East Side Gallery, the largest open-air gallery in the world, and covers 1.3 km of the Berlin Wall. The route includes the famous murals painted by international artists, including the famous "Fraternal Kiss" by Dmitri Vrubel, the "Brezhnev and Honecker" mural, and many others. The walk also covers the Oberbaum Bridge, the iconic structure that connects the districts of Friedrichshain and Kreuzberg, and the Spree River promenade, with its stunning views of the city skyline.

Walk length and cost:

The walk is approximately 1.3 km long and takes approximately 1 hour to complete. The cost is free, although a small fee may be charged for the services of a tour guide.

Meeting location and transportation:

The meeting location is at the East Side Gallery, located at Mühlenstraße, 10243 Berlin, Germany. The closest public transportation is the Warschauer Straße U-Bahn station, served by lines U1 and U3. From the station, it is a 5-minute walk to the East Side Gallery.

Historical background:

The East Side Gallery is a section of the Berlin Wall that was painted by artists from all over the world in 1990, just after the fall of the wall. It is a symbol of hope, freedom, and unity and has become one of Berlin's most popular tourist attractions.

Highlights and must-sees:

Some of the highlights and must-sees along this walk include the famous "Fraternal Kiss" mural, the "Brezhnev and Honecker" mural, the Oberbaum Bridge, and the Spree River promenade with its stunning views of the city skyline.

Curiosity and facts:

Did you know that the East Side Gallery is the largest open-air gallery in the world? It is also one of the few remaining sections of the Berlin Wall and serves as a reminder of the city's history and the events that led to its eventual reunification.

Advice:

Wear comfortable shoes and bring a camera to capture the stunning murals and views along the way. It is also recommended to bring a bottle of water and sunblock, especially during the summer months. Don't forget to take a break and enjoy a coffee or a snack at one of the many cafes and restaurants along the way.

Getting there:

To get to the East Side Gallery from the Warschauer Straße U-Bahn station, exit the station and turn right onto Wischerstra, walk straight ahead until you reach Mühlenstraße and turn left.Continue walking down Mühlenstraße until you reach the East Side Gallery, located on your right side.

Nearby attractions:

Some of the nearby attractions to the East Side Gallery include the Berlin Wall Memorial, the Spree River promenade, the Friedrichshain district, and the Oberbaum Bridge. Additionally, the famous Museum Island and Alexanderplatz are just a short distance away and can be easily reached by public transportation.

KIDS

KID IN BERLIN

Address: Berlin Zoo, Hardenbergplatz 8, 10623 Berlin, Germany.

Phone: +49 30 254010.

Child-friendly activities and attractions: Berlin Zoo, Legoland Discovery Centre Berlin, SEA LIFE Berlin, Botanical Garden, Trickfilm-Museum Stuttgart, Natural History Museum, Science Center Spectrum, Children's Museum, Planetarium, Wax Museum.

Food options: Berlin Zoo has a variety of food options for children, including snacks, light bites, and full meals.

Historical background: Berlin Zoo was founded in 1844 and is the oldest zoo in Germany. It is also one of the most popular tourist attractions in Berlin, attracting millions of visitors every year.

Highlights and must-sees: The highlights of Berlin Zoo include its diverse range of animals, from exotic primates to majestic elephants, as well as its beautiful landscaped gardens and historic architecture.

Curiosity and facts: Berlin Zoo is home to over 20,000 animals and is one of the largest zoos in the world. It is also a leading center for conservation and research, working to protect endangered species and their habitats.

Advice: To make the most of your visit to Berlin Zoo, it is recommended to arrive early and plan your route in advance. Wear comfortable shoes and dress for the weather, as the zoo is quite large and can take several hours to explore.

Getting there: Berlin Zoo is easily accessible by public transportation. The nearest metro station is Zoologischer Garten, which is served by several lines including U2, U9, and U7. From the station, it is a short walk to the zoo entrance.

Nearby attractions: Other popular attractions near Berlin Zoo include the Botanical Garden, the Natural History Museum, and the Science Center Spectrum.

LEGOLAND DISCOVERY CENTRE BERLIN

Address: Potsdamer Str. 4, 10785 Berlin, Germany.

Phone: +49 30 30013201.

Child-friendly activities and attractions: Legoland Discovery Centre Berlin is a child-friendly indoor attraction with a range of interactive and hands-on activities, including building challenges, interactive displays, and rides.

Food options: Legoland Discovery Centre Berlin has a cafe on site, serving a range of snacks and light bites.

Historical background: Legoland Discovery Centre Berlin is a chain of indoor attractions based on the popular Lego toy brand. The Berlin location opened in 2007 and has since become a popular destination for families with young children.

Highlights and must-sees: The highlights of Legoland Discovery Centre Berlin include its hands-on building activities, interactive displays, and rides, as well as its themed areas, such as the Lego Ninjago City Adventure and the Lego Friends Heartlake City.

Curiosity and facts: Legoland Discovery Centre Berlin is one of several locations worldwide, each offering a unique and interactive experience for children. It is also the only Legoland Discovery Centre in Germany.

Advice: To make the most of your visit to Legoland Discovery Centre Berlin, it is recommended to book your tickets in advance, as the attraction can get very busy, especially during peak times. Wear comfortable shoes and dress for the indoor climate.

Getting there: Legoland Discovery Centre Berlin is easily accessible by public transportation. The nearest metro station is Potsdamer Platz, which is served by several lines including U2, S1, and S25. From the station, it is a short walk to the attraction.

Nearby attractions: Other popular attractions near Legoland Discovery Centre Berlin include the Berlin Zoo, SEA LIFE Berlin, and the Botanical Garden.

SEA LIFE BERLIN

Address: Spandauer Str. 3, 10178 Berlin, Germany.

Phone: +49 30 2026030.

Child-friendly activities and attractions: SEA LIFE Berlin is a child-friendly indoor aquarium with a range of marine life and interactive displays, including a touch tank, a 360-degree ocean tunnel, and a sea turtle rescue center.

Food options: SEA LIFE Berlin has a cafe on site, serving a range of snacks and light bites.

Historical background: SEA LIFE Berlin is part of a chain of aquariums worldwide, each offering a unique and educational experience for visitors. The Berlin location opened in 2008 and has since become a popular destination for families with young children.

Highlights and must-sees: The highlights of SEA LIFE Berlin include its diverse range of marine life, including tropical fish, sea turtles, rays, and sharks, as well as its interactive displays, such as the touch tank and the 360-degree ocean tunnel.

Curiosity and facts: SEA LIFE Berlin is dedicated to educating visitors about the importance of ocean conservation and the protection of marine life. It is also a rescue center for injured sea turtles and is involved in several conservation projects worldwide.

Advice: To make the most of your visit to SEA LIFE Berlin, it is recommended to book your tickets in advance, as the attraction can get very busy, especially during peak times. Wear comfortable shoes and dress for the indoor climate.

Getting there: SEA LIFE Berlin is easily accessible by public transportation. The nearest metro station is Alexanderplatz, which is served by several lines including U2, U5, and U8. From the station, it is a short walk to the attraction.

Nearby attractions: Other popular attractions near SEA LIFE Berlin include the Berlin Zoo, Legoland Discovery Centre Berlin, and the Botanical Garden.

BOTANICAL GARDEN

Address: Königin-Luise-Str. 6-8, 14195 Berlin, Germany.

Phone: +49 30 83850.

Child-friendly activities and attractions: Botanical Garden is a child-friendly outdoor attraction with a range of botanical displays, including greenhouses, gardens, and nature trails.

Food options: Botanical Garden has a cafe on site, serving a range of snacks and light bites.

Historical background: Botanical Garden was founded in 1679 and is one of the oldest botanical gardens in the world. It is also one of the largest, with over 22,000 plant species and a rich history of scientific research and exploration.

Highlights and must-sees: The highlights of Botanical Garden include its diverse range of botanical displays, including greenhouses, gardens, and nature trails, as well as its historic architecture and beautiful landscaped grounds.

Curiosity and facts: Botanical Garden is home to a wide range of plant species, including many rare and exotic specimens. It is also a center for scientific research and education, with a focus on conservation and sustainable horticulture.

Advice: To make the most of your visit to Botanical Garden, it is recommended to arrive early and plan your route in advance. Wear comfortable shoes and dress for the weather, as the garden is quite large and can take several hours to explore.

Getting there: Botanical Garden is easily accessible by public transportation. The nearest metro station is Dahlem-Dorf, which is served by the U3 line. From the station, it is a short walk to the garden entrance.

Nearby attractions: Other popular attractions near Botanical Garden include the Berlin Zoo, Legoland Discovery Centre Berlin, and SEA LIFE Berlin.

TRICKFILM-MUSEUM STUTTGART

Address: Konrad-Adenauer-Str. 69, 70173 Stuttgart, Germany.

Phone: +49 711 97070.

Child-friendly activities and attractions: Trickfilm-Museum Stuttgart is a child-friendly indoor museum dedicated to the art of animation and special effects. It features a range of interactive displays and hands-on activities.

Food options: Trickfilm-Museum Stuttgart has a cafe on site, serving a range of snacks and light bites.

Historical background: Trickfilm-Museum Stuttgart is one of the largest museums dedicated to animation and special effects in Europe. It was founded in 1986 and has since become a popular destination for families with young children and animation enthusiasts.

Highlights and must-sees: The highlights of Trickfilm-Museum Stuttgart include its interactive displays and hands-on activities, as well as its collection of original animation artifacts and special effects equipment.

Curiosity and facts: Trickfilm-Museum Stuttgart is dedicated to preserving and promoting the art of animation and special effects, and is involved in several educational programs and events for children and adults.

Advice: To make the most of your visit to Trickfilm-Museum Stuttgart, it is recommended to book your tickets in advance, as the museum can get very busy, especially during peak times. Wear comfortable shoes and dress for the indoor climate.

Getting there: Trickfilm-Museum Stuttgart is easily accessible by public transportation. The nearest train station is Stuttgart Central Station, which is served by several lines including the S1, S2, and S3. From the station, it is a short walk or tram ride to the museum.

Nearby attractions: Other popular attractions near Trickfilm-Museum Stuttgart include the Natural History Museum and the Science Center Spectrum.

NATURAL HISTORY MUSEUM

Address: Rosenstein 1, 70191 Stuttgart, Germany.

Phone: +49 711 893640.

Child-friendly activities and attractions: Natural History Museum is a child-friendly indoor museum with a range of interactive displays and hands-on activities, including a dinosaur exhibit and a nature trail.

Food options: Natural History Museum has a cafe on site, serving a range of snacks and light bites.

Historical background: Natural History Museum was founded in 1823 and is one of the oldest natural history museums in Germany. It is also one of the largest, with a diverse collection of specimens and artifacts related to the natural world.

Highlights and must-sees: The highlights of Natural History Museum include its interactive displays, hands-on activities, and dinosaur exhibit, as well as its collection of specimens and artifacts related to the natural world, including fossils, minerals, and insects.

Curiosity and facts: Natural History Museum is a leading center for research and education in the natural sciences, with a focus on the preservation and interpretation of the natural world.

Advice: To make the most of your visit to Natural History Museum, it is recommended to book your tickets in advance, as the museum can get very busy, especially during peak times. Wear comfortable shoes and dress for the indoor climate.

Getting there: Natural History Museum is easily accessible by public transportation. The nearest train station is Stuttgart Central Station, which is served by several lines including the S1, S2, and S3. From the station, it is a short walk or tram ride to the museum.

Nearby attractions: Other popular attractions near Natural History Museum include the Trickfilm-Museum Stuttgart and the Science Center Spectrum.

SCIENCE CENTER SPECTRUM

Address: Pfaffenwaldring 5, 70569 Stuttgart, Germany.

Phone: +49 711 686980.

Child-friendly activities and attractions: Science Center Spectrum is a child-friendly indoor science center with a range of interactive displays and hands-on activities, including experiments, demonstrations, and simulations.

Food options: Science Center Spectrum has a cafe on site, serving a range of snacks and light bites.

Historical background: Science Center Spectrum was founded in 1979 and is one of the largest science centers in Germany. It is dedicated to promoting scientific literacy and education, and offers a range of interactive displays and hands-on activities for visitors of all ages.

Highlights and must-sees: The highlights of Science Center Spectrum include its interactive displays and hands-on activities, as well as its planetarium and its collection of scientific specimens and artifacts.

Curiosity and facts: Science Center Spectrum is involved in a range of scientific research and education programs, including partnerships with universities and research institutions.

Advice: To make the most of your visit to Science Center Spectrum, it is recommended to book your tickets in advance, as the center can get very busy, especially during peak times. Wear comfortable shoes and dress for the indoor climate.

Getting there: Science Center Spectrum is easily accessible by public transportation. The nearest train station is Stuttgart Central Station, which is served by several lines including the S1, S2, and S3. From the station, it is a short walk or tram ride to the center.

Nearby attractions: Other popular attractions near Science Center Spectrum include the Trickfilm-Museum Stuttgart and the Natural History Museum.

CHILDREN'S MUSEUM

Address: Address: Wallstraße 14, 10179 Berlin, Germany.

Phone: +49 30 24749 796.

Child-friendly activities and attractions: Children's Museum is a child-friendly indoor museum with a range of interactive displays and hands-on activities, designed specifically for young children.

Food options: Children's Museum has a cafe on site, serving a range of snacks and light bites.

Historical background: Children's Museum was founded in 2003 and is dedicated to providing a fun and educational experience for young children. It is one of the few museums in Berlin specifically designed for children.

Highlights and must-sees: The highlights of Children's Museum include its interactive displays and hands-on activities, as well as its collection of educational materials and resources for families with young children.

Curiosity and facts: Children's Museum is involved in several educational programs and events for young children, including workshops, classes, and family activities.

Advice: To make the most of your visit to Children's Museum, it is recommended to book your tickets in advance, as the museum can get very busy, especially during peak times. Wear comfortable shoes and dress for the indoor climate.

Getting there: Children's Museum is easily accessible by public transportation. The nearest metro station is Märkisches Museum, which is served by the U2 line. From the station, it is a short walk to the museum.

Nearby attractions: Other popular attractions near Children's Museum include the Planetarium, the Wax Museum, and the Berlin Zoo.

PLANETARIUM

Address: Prenzlauer Allee 80, 10405 Berlin, Germany.

Phone: +49 30 6663 6200.

Child-friendly activities and attractions: Planetarium is a child-friendly indoor attraction with a range of interactive displays and hands-on activities, as well as a planetarium show.

Food options: Planetarium has a cafe on site, serving a range of snacks and light bites.

Historical background: Planetarium was founded in 1987 and is dedicated to promoting scientific literacy and education, with a focus on astronomy and space science.

Highlights and must-sees: The highlights of Planetarium include its interactive displays, hands-on activities, and planetarium show, as well as its collection of scientific specimens and artifacts related to astronomy and space science.

Curiosity and facts: Planetarium is a leading center for research and education in astronomy and space science, and is involved in several educational programs and events for children and adults.

Advice: To make the most of your visit to Planetarium, it is recommended to book your tickets in advance, as the attraction can get very busy, especially during peak times. Wear comfortable shoes and dress for the indoor climate.

Getting there: Planetarium is easily accessible by public transportation. The nearest metro station is EberswalderStraße, which is served by the U2 line. From the station, it is a short walk to the planetarium.

Nearby attractions: Other popular attractions near Planetarium include the Children's Museum, the Wax Museum, and the Berlin Zoo.

WAX MUSEUM

Address: Unter den Linden 74, 10117 Berlin, Germany.

Phone: +49 30 2045 8900.

Child-friendly activities and attractions: Wax Museum is a child-friendly indoor attraction with a range of life-like wax figures, including historical figures, celebrities, and fictional characters.

Food options: Wax Museum has a cafe on site, serving a range of snacks and light bites.

Historical background: Wax Museum was founded in 1963 and is one of the oldest wax museums in Europe. It is dedicated to preserving and promoting the art of wax figure-making, and is home to a collection of over 200 life-like wax figures.

Highlights and must-sees: The highlights of Wax Museum include its life-like wax figures, including historical figures, celebrities, and fictional characters, as well as its collection of wax-making artifacts and tools.

Curiosity and facts: Wax Museum is involved in several educational programs and events, including workshops and classes on the art of wax figure-making.

Advice: To make the most of your visit to Wax Museum, it is recommended to book your tickets in advance, as the museum can get very busy, especially during peak times. Wear comfortable shoes and dress for the indoor climate.

Getting there: Wax Museum is easily accessible by public transportation. The nearest metro station is Unter den Linden, which is served by the S5, S7, and S75 lines. From the station, it is a short walk to the museum.

Nearby attractions: Other popular attractions near Wax Museum include the Planetarium, the Children's Museum, and the Berlin Zoo.

RESTAURANTS

VÖNER

Address: Flughafenstraße 46, 12053 Berlin, Germany.

Phone: +49 30 1234567

Hours of operation: Mon-Sun: 11:00 AM- 9:00 PM

Cost score: $$

Menu and cuisine: Vöner is a vegan kebab restaurant that serves plant-based meat alternatives, salads, sauces, and sides.

Atmosphere and ambiance: The restaurant has a relaxed, casual atmosphere with a modern interior design and comfortable seating.

Services and amenities: Vöner offers dine-in, take-out, and delivery services. They also have free Wi-Fi and outdoor seating.

Reviews and ratings: Vöner has received positive reviews for their delicious food and great service. They have an average rating of 4.5 stars on various websites.

Historical background: Vöner is a relatively new restaurant in Berlin, having opened its doors in the past few years.

Curiosity and facts: Vöner is known for its innovative approach to vegan cuisine, using plant-based meat alternatives to create traditional kebab dishes.

Advice: Try the Vöner Kebab with a side of their famous garlic sauce.

Getting there: Vöner is located in the heart of Berlin and can be easily reached by metro. Take the U1 line to the OranienburgerStraße station and walk 5 minutes to the restaurant.

Nearby attractions: Some popular attractions near Vöner include Checkpoint Charlie Museum, Brandenburg Gate, and the Berlin Wall Memorial.

MARKTHALLE NEUN

Address: Eisenbahnstraße 42/43, 10997 Berlin, Germany.

Phone: +49 30 7654321

Hours of operation: Mon-Sun: 10:00 AM- 10:00 PM

Cost score: $$$

Menu and cuisine: Markthalle Neun is a food market that offers a variety of international cuisines including Mediterranean, Asian, and German dishes.

Atmosphere and ambiance: The market has a lively and bustling atmosphere, with vendors selling fresh produce and a range of prepared foods.

Services and amenities: Markthalle Neun offers dine-in, take-out, and delivery services. They also have free Wi-Fi and outdoor seating.

Reviews and ratings: Markthalle Neun is highly rated for its diverse food offerings and lively atmosphere. They have an average rating of 4.7 stars on various websites.

Historical background: Markthalle Neun has been a staple in Berlin for over a century, originally serving as a market for local farmers to sell their produce.

Curiosity and facts: Markthalle Neun is known for its street food scene, hosting events like the Street Food

Thursday where food vendors from around the world gather to sell their signature dishes.

Advice: Try the fresh seafood at the Fischmarkt or the Asian street food at the Wok Show.

Getting there: Markthalle Neun is located in the Kreuzberg neighborhood of Berlin and can be easily reached by metro. Take the U1 line to the Kottbusser Tor station and walk 10 minutes to the market.

Nearby attractions: Some popular attractions near Markthalle Neun include the East Side Gallery, the Berlin Wall Memorial, and the Görlitzer Park.

STREET FOOD THURSDAY

Address: Straße der Pariser Kommune, Berlin, Germany.

Phone: +49 30 1111111

Hours of operation: Thu: 5:00 PM- 10:00 PM

Cost score: $-$$

Menu and cuisine: Street Food Thursday is an outdoor food market that offers a variety of international street food, including tacos, burgers, and street-style seafood.

Atmosphere and ambiance: The market has a lively and energetic atmosphere, with food vendors, live music, and a bustling crowd.

Services and amenities: Street Food Thursday offers take-out and street-side seating. They also have free Wi-Fi and an ATM on site.

Reviews and ratings: Street Food Thursday is highly rated for its diverse food offerings and festive atmosphere. They have an average rating of 4.8 stars on various websites.

Historical background: Street Food Thursday has been a popular event in Berlin for several years, attracting foodies and locals alike to sample a range of international street food.

Curiosity and facts: Street Food Thursday is known for its rotating lineup of food vendors, ensuring that there is always something new and exciting to try.

Advice: Try the Thai street food at the Pad Thai stand or the Mexican street tacos at the Taco Truck.

Getting there: Street Food Thursday is located in the heart of Berlin and can be easily reached by metro. Take the U1 line to the Alexanderplatz station and walk 5 minutes to the market.

Nearby attractions: Some popular attractions near Street Food Thursday include the Berlin TV Tower, the Nikolaiviertelneighborhood, and the Berlin Wall Memorial.

KONNOPKE'S IMBISS

Address: Schönhauser Allee 44b, 10435 Berlin, Germany.

Phone: +49 30 2222222

Hours of operation: Mon-Sun: 10:00 AM- 8:00 PM

Cost score: $

Menu and cuisine: Konnopke'sImbiss is a traditional German street food stand, serving up classic dishes like currywurst and schnitzel sandwiches.

Atmosphere and ambiance: The stand has a no-frills, fast-food vibe, with a counter for ordering and outdoor seating available.

Services and amenities: Konnopke'sImbiss offers take-out only, with no dine-in options available.

Reviews and ratings: Konnopke'sImbiss is highly rated for its authentic German street food and reasonable prices. They have an average rating of 4.3 stars on various websites.

Historical background: Konnopke'sImbiss has been a staple in Berlin for over 80 years, originally serving as a food cart for workers during World War II.

Curiosity and facts: Konnopke'sImbissis known for its famous currywurst, made with a secret family recipe passed down through generations.

Advice: Try the classic currywurst with a side of pommes (fries) and a soda.

Getting there: Konnopke'sImbiss is located in the Prenzlauer Berg neighborhood of Berlin and can be easily reached by metro. Take the U2 line to the EberswalderStraße station and walk 5 minutes to the stand.

Nearby attractions: Some popular attractions near Konnopke'sImbiss include the Mauerpark, the Kulturbrauerei cultural center, and the Prenzlauer Berg neighborhood.

CURRY 36

Address: Mehringdamm 36, 10961 Berlin, Germany.

Phone: +49 30 3333333

Hours of operation: Mon-Sun: 11:00 AM- 10:00 PM

Cost score: $

Menu and cuisine: Curry 36 is a German street food stand specializing in currywurst, serving up a range of variations with different sauces and toppings.

Atmosphere and ambiance: The stand has a fast-food vibe, with a counter for ordering and outdoor seating available.

Services and amenities: Curry 36 offers take-out only, with no dine-in options available.

Reviews and ratings: Curry 36 is highly rated for its delicious currywurst and affordable prices. They have an average rating of 4.5 stars on various websites.

Historical background: Curry 36 has been a popular street food destination in Berlin for several years, serving up classic German cuisine with a modern twist.

Curiosity and facts: Curry 36 is known for its unique curry sauces, made with a secret blend of spices and ingredients.

Advice: Try the classic currywurst with a side of pommes (fries) and a drink of your choice.

Getting there: Curry 36 is located in the heart of Berlin and can be easily reached by metro. Take the U1 line to the Kurfürstendamm station and walk 5 minutes to the stand.

Nearby attractions: Some popular attractions near Curry 36 include the KaDeWe department store, the Berlin Zoo, and the Europa-Center shopping mall.

IMREN GRILL

Address: Neue Schönhauser Str. 16, 10178 Berlin, Germany.

Phone: +49 30 4444444

Hours of operation: Mon-Sun: 11:00 AM- 10:00 PM

Cost score: $$

Menu and cuisine: Imren Grill is a Turkish restaurant that specializes in grilled meat dishes, including kebabs, shish tavuk (chicken skewers), and adana kebabs (spicy minced meat skewers).

Atmosphere and ambiance: The restaurant has a warm and inviting atmosphere, with a traditional Turkish interior and comfortable seating.

Services and amenities: Imren Grill offers dine-in, take-out, and delivery services. They also have free Wi-Fi and outdoor seating.

Reviews and ratings: Imren Grill is highly rated for its delicious food and authentic Turkish cuisine. They have an average rating of 4.7 stars on various websites.

Historical background: Imren Grill is a relatively new restaurant in Berlin, having opened its doors in the past few years.

Curiosity and facts: Imren Grill is known for its juicy and flavorful kebabs, cooked over an open flame for a smoky, grilled taste.

Advice: Try the adana kebab with a side of bulgur pilaf and ayran (Turkish yogurt drink).

Getting there: Imren Grill is located in the Neuköllnneighborhood of Berlin and can be easily reached by metro. Take the U7 line to the Neukölln station and walk 5 minutes to the restaurant.

Nearby attractions: Some popular attractions near Imren Grill include the Kreuzberg neighborhood, the Tempelhofer Park, and the NeuköllnArcaden shopping mall.

MUSTAFA'S GEMÜSE KEBAB

Address: Mehringdamm 32, 10961 Berlin, Germany.

Phone: +49 30 5555555

Hours of operation: Mon-Sun: 11:00 AM- 10:00 PM

Cost score: $

Menu and cuisine: Mustafa's Gemüse Kebab is a vegetarian kebab stand that serves up delicious meat-free kebabs, made with a range of fresh vegetables and sauces.

Atmosphere and ambiance: The stand has a casual and relaxed atmosphere, with a counter for ordering and outdoor seating available.

Services and amenities: Mustafa's Gemüse Kebab offers take-out only, with no dine-in options available.

Reviews and ratings: Mustafa's Gemüse Kebab is highly rated for its tasty and healthy food options. They have an average rating of 4.6 stars on various websites.

Historical background: Mustafa's Gemüse Kebab has been a popular food destination in Berlin for several years, offering a vegetarian alternative to traditional kebab stands.

Curiosity and facts: Mustafa's Gemüse Kebab is known for its creative and flavorful kebab combinations, made with a range of fresh vegetables and sauces.

Advice: Try the falafel kebab with a side of hummus and pita bread.

Getting there: Mustafa's Gemüse Kebab is located in the Friedrichshainneighborhood of Berlin and can be easily reached by metro. Take the U5 line to the Frankfurter Allee station and walk 5 minutes to the stand.

Nearby attractions: Some popular attractions near Mustafa's Gemüse Kebab include the East Side Gallery, the Simon-Dach-Straßeneighborhood, and the Boxhagener Platz park.

YOYO FOOD WORLD

Address: Flughafenstraße 46, 12053 Berlin, Germany.

Phone: +49 30 6666666

Hours of operation: Mon-Sun: 11:00 AM- 10:00 PM

Cost score: $$

Menu and cuisine: Yoyo Food World is a fusion restaurant that serves up a range of international dishes, including Thai curries, Mexican tacos, and Italian pasta.

Atmosphere and ambiance: The restaurant has a modern and trendy atmosphere, with a stylish interior and comfortable seating.

Services and amenities: Yoyo Food World offers dine-in, take-out, and delivery services. They also have free Wi-Fi and outdoor seating.

Reviews and ratings: Yoyo Food World is highly rated for its creative and delicious food options. They have an average rating of 4.8 stars on various websites.

Historical background: Yoyo Food World is a relatively new restaurant in Berlin, having opened its doors in the past few years.

Curiosity and facts: Yoyo Food World is known for its unique and innovative dishes, combining flavors and ingredients from around the world.

Advice: Try the green curry with jasmine rice and a side of spring rolls.

Getting there: Yoyo Food World is located in the Mitte neighborhood of Berlin and can be easily reached by metro. Take the U8 line to the Alexanderplatz station and walk 10 minutes to the restaurant.

Nearby attractions: Some popular attractions near Yoyo Food World include the Berlin Wall Museum, the Brandenburg Gate, and the Museum Island.

CHIMICHURRI

Address: Mainzer Str. 23, 10247 Berlin, Germany.

Phone: +49 30 7777777

Hours of operation: Mon-Sun: 12:00 PM- 9:00 PM

Cost score: $$

Menu and cuisine: Chimichurri is an Argentinean steakhouse that serves up a range of grilled meat dishes, including steaks, sausages, and mixed grills.

Atmosphere and ambiance: The restaurant has a warm and inviting atmosphere, with a traditional Argentinean interior and comfortable seating.

Services and amenities: Chimichurri offers dine-in, take-out, and delivery services. They also have free Wi-Fi and outdoor seating.

Reviews and ratings: Chimichurri is highly rated for its juicy and flavorful steaks and authentic Argentinean cuisine. They have an average rating of 4.9 stars on various websites.

Historical background: Chimichurri is a relatively new restaurant in Berlin, having opened its doors in the past few years.

Curiosity and facts: Chimichurri is known for its famous chimichurri sauce, a tangy and flavorful blend of herbs and spices that is the perfect accompaniment to grilled meat dishes.

Advice: Try the bife de chorizo (sirloin steak) with chimichurri sauce and a side of roasted potatoes.

Getting there: Chimichurri is located in the Prenzlauer Berg neighborhood of Berlin and can be easily reached by metro. Take the U2 line to the Senefelderplatz station and walk 5 minutes to the restaurant.

Nearby attractions: Some popular attractions near Chimichurri include the Mauerpark, the Kulturbrauerei cultural center, and the EberswalderStraße shopping street.

SHISO BURGER

Address: Alte Schönhauser Str. 46, 10119 Berlin, Germany.

Phone: +49 30 8888888

Hours of operation: Mon-Sun: 11:00 AM- 10:00 PM

Cost score: $

Menu and cuisine: Shiso Burger is a fast food restaurant that specializes in burgers, made with fresh ingredients and unique flavor combinations.

Atmosphere and ambiance: The restaurant has a casual and relaxed atmosphere, with a modern interior and comfortable seating.

Services and amenities: Shiso Burger offers dine-in, take-out, and delivery services. They also have free Wi-Fi and outdoor seating.

Reviews and ratings: Shiso Burger is highly rated for its tasty and creative burgers. They have an average rating of 4.7 stars on various websites.

Historical background: Shiso Burger is a relatively new restaurant in Berlin, having opened its doors in the past few years.

Curiosity and facts: Shiso Burger is known for its unique burger toppings, including the shiso leaf, a fragrant and flavorful herb used in Asian cuisine.

Advice: Try the shiso burger with a side of sweet potato fries and a drink of your choice.

Getting there: Shiso Burger is located in the Kreuzberg neighborhood of Berlin and can be easily reached by metro. Take the U1 line to the Kottbusser Tor station and walk 5 minutes to the restaurant.

Nearby attractions: Some popular attractions near Shiso Burger include the Kreuzberg neighborhood, the Landwehrkanal canal, and the Admiralbrücke bridge.

NIGHTLIFE

BERGHAIN

Address: Am WriezenerBahnhof, 10243 Berlin, Germany.

Phone: +49 30 29360210

Hours of operation: Fridays and Saturdays from midnight to noon and sometimes even later.

Cost score: €€€

Drinks and menu: Berghain is famous for its extensive selection of techno music, as well as its high-quality drinks and food. The menu includes a wide range of cocktails, beers, and non-alcoholic drinks, as well as snacks and light bites.

Atmosphere and ambiance: The atmosphere at Berghain is one of darkness, intensity, and energy. The club is known for its dim lighting and intense techno music, which creates an intense and exciting atmosphere that is perfect for dancing the night away.

Entertainment and events: Berghain is one of the most famous techno clubs in the world, and is known for hosting some of the biggest techno music events and parties. The club is also home to a number of international DJs and musicians, who perform regularly and keep the party going all night long.

Reviews and ratings: Berghain is widely regarded as one of the best nightclubs in the world, with many rave reviews and high ratings from guests who have visited the club. The club is known for its intense atmosphere, high-quality drinks and food, and its world-renowned music events.

Historical background: Berghain was founded in 2004, and has since become one of the most famous techno clubs in the world. The club is housed in a former power plant, which adds to its dark and intense atmosphere.

Curiosity and facts: Berghain is known for its strict door policy, with many guests being turned away by the club's infamous bouncers. The club is also famous for its long opening hours, with parties lasting for up to 20 hours at a time.

Advice: If you're planning to visit Berghain, be sure to dress appropriately, as the club has a strict dress code. It's also important to be prepared for the intense atmosphere and loud music, which can be overwhelming for some guests.

Getting there: Berghain is located in the Friedrichshainneighborhood of Berlin, and can be easily reached by metro. The nearest metro station is Warschauer Straße, which is just a few minutes' walk from the club.

Nearby attractions: Some nearby attractions include the East Side Gallery, the Berlin Wall Memorial, and the Berlin Wall Museum.

WATERGATE

Address: Falckensteinstr. 49, 10997 Berlin, Germany.

Phone: +49 30 61283971

Hours of operation: Watergate is open Wednesday through Sunday, from 11 PM to late.

Cost score: €€

Drinks and menu: Watergate offers a wide range of high-quality drinks, including cocktails, beers, and non-alcoholic beverages. The club also has a bar menu, with a variety of snacks and light bites available.

Atmosphere and ambiance: The atmosphere at Watergate is relaxed and laid-back, with a focus on good music, good drinks, and good vibes. The club has a spacious outdoor terrace, which provides a great place to take a break from the music and enjoy the views over the river.

Entertainment and events: Watergate is known for hosting a variety of music events, including techno, house, and electronic dance music. The club also features live performances by local and international DJs and musicians.

Reviews and ratings: Watergate has received positive reviews from guests, who appreciate the club's relaxed atmosphere and great music. The club is known for its high-quality drinks, friendly staff, and its stunning location on the river.

Historical background: Watergate was founded in 2002 and has since become one of Berlin's most popular nightclubs. The club is located on the river Spree, in the heart of Berlin, and is housed in a modern building with stunning views of the city.

Curiosity and facts: Watergate is known for its iconic light-up dance floor, which adds to the club's relaxed and fun atmosphere. The club also has a spacious outdoor terrace, which provides a great place to relax and enjoy the views over the river.

Advice: If you're planning to visit Watergate, be sure to dress comfortably, as the club has a relaxed dress code. It's also important to arrive early, as the club can get busy later in the night.

Getting there: Watergate is located in the Kreuzberg neighborhood of Berlin, and can be easily reached by metro. The nearest metro station is Warschauer Straße, which is just a short walk from the club.

Nearby attractions: Some nearby attractions include the East Side Gallery, the Berlin Wall Memorial, and the Berlin Wall Museum.

TRESOR

Address: Köpenicker Str. 70, 10179 Berlin, Germany.

Phone: +49 30 29362362

Hours of operation: Tresor is open Thursday through Sunday, from 11 PM to late.

Cost score: €€

Drinks and menu: Tresor offers a wide range of high-quality drinks, including cocktails, beers, and non-alcoholic beverages. The club also has a bar menu, with a variety of snacks and light bites available.

Atmosphere and ambiance: Tresor is known for its dark and intense atmosphere, with a focus on techno music and high-energy parties. The club features a large dance floor and powerful sound system, which creates an electrifying atmosphere for dancing the night away.

Entertainment and events: Tresor is one of Berlin's most famous techno clubs, and is known for hosting some of the biggest techno music events in the city. The club features a rotating line-up of international DJs and musicians, who perform regularly and keep the party going all night long.

Reviews and ratings: Tresor has received positive reviews from guests, who appreciate the club's intense atmosphere and great music. The club is known for its high-quality drinks, friendly staff, and its electrifying parties.

Historical background: Tresor was founded in 1991 and is one of the oldest and most famous techno clubs in Berlin. The club is housed in a former underground vault, which adds to its dark and intense atmosphere.

Curiosity and facts: Tresor is known for its strict door policy, with many guests being turned away by the club's bouncers. The club is also famous for its long opening hours, with parties lasting for up to 20 hours at a time.

Advice: If you're planning to visit Tresor, be sure to dress appropriately, as the club has a strict dress code. It's also important to be prepared for the intense atmosphere and loud music, which can be overwhelming for some guests.

Getting there: Tresor is located in the Mitte neighborhood of Berlin, and can be easily reached by metro. The nearest metro station is Warschauer Straße, which is just a short walk from the club.

Nearby attractions: Some nearby attractions include the Brandenburg Gate, the Reichstag Building, and the Berlin Wall Memorial.

SISYPHOS

Address: Hauptstraße 15, 10557 Berlin, Germany.

Phone: +49 30 39404794

Hours of operation: Sisyphos is open Thursday through Sunday, from 11 PM to late.

Cost score: €€€

Drinks and menu: Sisyphos offers a wide range of high-quality drinks, including cocktails, beers, and non-alcoholic beverages. The club also has a bar menu, with a variety of snacks and light bites available.

Atmosphere and ambiance: The atmosphere at Sisyphos is relaxed and laid-back, with a focus on good music, good drinks, and good vibes. The club features a spacious outdoor area, which provides a great place to relax and enjoy the views over the river.

Entertainment and events: Sisyphos is known for hosting a variety of music events, including techno, house, and electronic dance music. The club also features live performances by local and international DJs and musicians.

Reviews and ratings: Sisyphos has received positive reviews from guests, who appreciate the club's relaxed atmosphere and great music. The club is known for its high-quality drinks, friendly staff, and its spacious outdoor area.

Historical background: Sisyphos was founded in 2015 and has since become one of Berlin's most popular nightclubs. The club is located in the Neuköllnneighborhood, and is housed in a large, modern building with a spacious outdoor area.

Curiosity and facts: Sisyphos is known for its eclectic mix of music and its relaxed atmosphere, which makes it a popular choice for both locals and tourists. The club also features a large outdoor area, which provides a great place to relax and enjoy the views over the river.

Advice: If you're planning to visit Sisyphos, be sure to dress comfortably, as the club has a relaxed dress code. It's also important to arrive early, as the club can get busy later in the night.

Getting there: Sisyphos is located in the Neuköllnneighborhood of Berlin, and can be easily reached by metro. The nearest metro station is Sonnenallee, which is just a short walk from the club.

Nearby attractions: Some nearby attractions include the Tempelhof Park, the NeuköllnArcaden shopping center, and the NeuköllnNeighborhood.

KATER BLAU

Address: Holzmarktstraße 25, 10243 Berlin, Germany.

Phone: +49 30 97007766

Hours of operation: Kater Blau is open Thursday through Sunday, from 11 PM to late.

Cost score: €€€

Drinks and menu: Kater Blau offers a wide range of high-quality drinks, including cocktails, beers, and non-alcoholic beverages. The club also has a bar menu, with a variety of snacks and light bites available.

Atmosphere and ambiance: The atmosphere at Kater Blau is relaxed and laid-back, with a focus on good music, good drinks, and good vibes. The club features a spacious outdoor terrace, which provides a great place to relax and enjoy the views over the river.

Entertainment and events: Kater Blau is known for hosting a variety of music events, including techno, house, and electronic dance music. The club also features live performances by local and international DJs and musicians.

Reviews and ratings: Kater Blau has received positive reviews from guests, who appreciate the club's relaxed atmosphere and great music. The club is known for its high-quality drinks, friendly staff, and its spacious outdoor terrace.

Historical background: Kater Blau was founded in 2013 and has since become one of Berlin's most popular nightclubs. The club is located in the Friedrichshainneighborhood, and is housed in a modern building with a spacious outdoor terrace.

Curiosity and facts: Kater Blau is known for its eclectic mix of music and its relaxed atmosphere, which makes it a popular choice for both locals and tourists. The club also features a large outdoor terrace, which provides a great place to relax and enjoy the views over the river.

Advice: If you're planning to visit Kater Blau, be sure to dress comfortably, as the club has a relaxed dress code. It's also important to arrive early, as the club can get busy later in the night.

Getting there: Kater Blau is located in the Friedrichshain neighborhood of Berlin, and can be easily reached by metro. The nearest metro station is Ostbahnhof, which is just a short walk from the club.

Nearby attractions: Some nearby attractions include the East Side Gallery, the Berlin Wall Memorial, and the Simon-Dach-Straße neighborhood.

CLUB DER VISIONAERE

Address: Am Flutgraben 1, 12435 Berlin, Germany.

Phone: +49 30 53151340

Hours of operation: Club der Visionaere is open Wednesday through Sunday, from 11 PM to late.

Cost score: €€€

Drinks and menu: Club der Visionaere offers a wide range of high-quality drinks, including cocktails, beers, and non-alcoholic beverages. The club also has a bar menu, with a variety of snacks and light bites available.

Atmosphere and ambiance: The atmosphere at Club der Visionaere is relaxed and laid-back, with a focus on good music, good drinks, and good vibes. The club features a spacious outdoor area, which provides a great place to relax and enjoy the views over the river.

Entertainment and events: Club der Visionaere is known for hosting a variety of music events, including techno, house, and electronic dance music. The club also features live performances by local and international DJs and musicians.

Reviews and ratings: Club der Visionaere has received positive reviews from guests, who appreciate the club's relaxed atmosphere and great music. The club is known for its high-quality drinks, friendly staff, and its spacious outdoor area.

Historical background: Club der Visionaere was founded in 1999 and has since become one of Berlin's most popular nightclubs. The club is located in the Kreuzberg neighborhood, and is housed in a modern building with a spacious outdoor area.

Curiosity and facts: Club der Visionaere is known for its relaxed atmosphere and its focus on techno and electronic dance music. The club is also famous for its large outdoor area, which provides a great place to relax and enjoy the views over the river.

Advice: If you're planning to visit Club der Visionaere, be sure to dress comfortably, as the club has a relaxed dress code. It's also important to arrive early, as the club can get busy later in the night.

Getting there: Club der Visionaere is located in the Kreuzberg neighborhood of Berlin, and can be easily reached by metro. The nearest metro station is Schlesisches Tor, which is just a short walk from the club.

Nearby attractions: Some nearby attractions include the East Side Gallery, the Berlin Wall Memorial, and the Simon-Dach-Straßeneighborhood.

RITTER

Address: Ritterstraße 26, 10969 Berlin, Germany.

Phone: +49 30 25762366

Hours of operation: Ritter is open Friday and Saturday, from 11 PM to late.

Cost score: €€€

Drinks and menu: Ritter offers a wide range of high-quality drinks, including cocktails, beers, and non-alcoholic beverages. The club also has a bar menu, with a variety of snacks and light bites available.

Atmosphere and ambiance: The atmosphere at Ritter is relaxed and laid-back, with a focus on good music, good drinks, and good vibes. The club features a spacious outdoor area, which provides a great place to relax and enjoy the views over the city.

Entertainment and events: Ritter is known for hosting a variety of music events, including techno, house, and electronic dance music. The club also features live performances by local and international DJs and musicians.

Reviews and ratings: Ritter has received positive reviews from guests, who appreciate the club's relaxed atmosphere and great music. The club is known for its high-quality drinks, friendly staff, and its spacious outdoor area.

Historical background: Ritter was founded in 2013 and has since become one of Berlin's most popular nightclubs. The club is located in the Kreuzberg neighborhood, and is housed in a modern building with a spacious outdoor area.

Curiosity and facts: Ritter is known for its relaxed atmosphere and its focus on techno and electronic dance music. The club is also famous for its large outdoor area, which provides a great place to relax and enjoy the views over the city.

Advice: If you're planning to visit Ritter, be sure to dress comfortably, as the club has a relaxed dress code. It's also important to arrive early, as the club can get busy later in the night.

Getting there: Ritter is located in the Kreuzberg neighborhood of Berlin, and can be easily reached by metro. The nearest metro station is Kottbusser Tor, which is just a short walk from the club.

Nearby attractions: Some nearby attractions include the East Side Gallery, the Berlin Wall Memorial, and the Simon-Dach-Straßeneighborhood.

CASSIOPEIA BERLIN

Address: Revaler Str. 99, 10245 Berlin, Germany.

Phone: +49 30 54919510

Hours of operation: Cassiopeia Berlin is open Wednesday through Sunday, from 11 PM to late.

Cost score: €€€

Drinks and menu: Cassiopeia Berlin offers a wide range of high-quality drinks, including cocktails, beers, and non-alcoholic beverages. The club also has a bar menu, with a variety of snacks and light bites available.

Atmosphere and ambiance: The atmosphere at Cassiopeia Berlin is relaxed and laid-back, with a focus on good music, good drinks, and good vibes. The club features a spacious outdoor area, which provides a great place to relax and enjoy the views over the city.

Entertainment and events: Cassiopeia Berlin is known for hosting a variety of music events, including rock, punk, and alternative music. The club also features live performances by local and international musicians and bands.

Reviews and ratings: Cassiopeia Berlin has received positive reviews from guests, who appreciate the club's relaxed atmosphere and great music. The club is known for its high-quality drinks, friendly staff, and its spacious outdoor area.

Historical background: Cassiopeia Berlin was founded in 2006 and has since become one of Berlin's most popular nightclubs for alternative music. The club is located in the Friedrichshainneighborhood, and is housed in a modern building with a spacious outdoor area.

Curiosity and facts: Cassiopeia Berlin is known for its relaxed atmosphere and its focus on alternative music. The club is also famous for its large outdoor area, which provides a great place to relax and enjoy the views over the city.

Advice: If you're planning to visit Cassiopeia Berlin, be sure to dress comfortably, as the club has a relaxed dress code. It's also important to arrive early, as the club can get busy later in the night.

Getting there: Cassiopeia Berlin is located in the Friedrichshainneighborhood of Berlin, and can be easily reached by metro. The nearest metro station is Warschauer Str., which is just a short walk from the club.

Nearby attractions: Some nearby attractions include the East Side Gallery, the Berlin Wall Memorial, and the Simon-Dach-Straßeneighborhood.

SO36

Address: Oranienstraße 190, 10999 Berlin, Germany.

Phone: +49 30 6165096

Hours of operation: SO36 is open Thursday through Saturday, from 11 PM to late.

Cost score: €€€

Drinks and menu: SO36 offers a wide range of high-quality drinks, including cocktails, beers, and non-alcoholic beverages. The club also has a bar menu, with a variety of snacks and light bites available.

Atmosphere and ambiance: The atmosphere at SO36 is relaxed and laid-back, with a focus on good music, good drinks, and good vibes. The club features a spacious outdoor area, which provides a great place to relax and enjoy the views over the city.

Entertainment and events: SO36 is known for hosting a variety of music events, including punk, alternative, and electronic dance music. The club also features live performances by local and international musicians and DJs.

Reviews and ratings: SO36 has received positive reviews from guests, who appreciate the club's relaxed atmosphere and great music. The club is known for its high-quality drinks, friendly staff, and its spacious outdoor area.

Historical background: SO36 was founded in 1978 and has since become one of Berlin's most popular nightclubs for punk and alternative music. The club is located in the Kreuzberg neighborhood, and is housed in a modern building with a spacious outdoor area.

Curiosity and facts: SO36 is known for its relaxed atmosphere and its focus on punk and alternative music. The club is also famous for its large outdoor area, which provides a great place to relax and enjoy the views over the city.

Advice: If you're planning to visit SO36, be sure to dress comfortably, as the club has a relaxed dress code. It's also important to arrive early, as the club can get busy later in the night.

Getting there: SO36 is located in the Kreuzberg neighborhood of Berlin, and can be easily reached by metro. The nearest metro station is Kottbusser Tor, which is just a short walk from the club.

Nearby attractions: Some nearby attractions include the East Side Gallery, the Berlin Wall Memorial, and the Simon-Dach-Straßeneighborhood.

GRIESSMÜHLE

Address: Sonnenallee 221, 12059 Berlin, Germany.

Phone: +49 30 54797290

Hours of operation: Griessmühle is open Thursday through Sunday, from 11 PM to late.

Cost score: €€€

Drinks and menu: Griessmühleoffers a wide range of high-quality drinks, including cocktails, beers, and non-alcoholic beverages. The club also has a bar menu, with a variety of snacks and light bites available.

Atmosphere and ambiance: The atmosphere at Griessmühle is relaxed and laid-back, with a focus on good music, good drinks, and good vibes. The club features a spacious outdoor area, which provides a great place to relax and enjoy the views over the city.

Entertainment and events: Griessmühle is known for hosting a variety of music events, including techno, house, and electronic dance music. The club also features live performances by local and international DJs and musicians.

Reviews and ratings: Griessmühlehas received positive reviews from guests, who appreciate the club's relaxed atmosphere and great music. The club is known for its high-quality drinks, friendly staff, and its spacious outdoor area.

Historical background: Griessmühle was founded in 2013 and has since become one of Berlin's most popular nightclubs. The club is located in the Neuköllnneighborhood, and is housed in a modern building with a spacious outdoor area.

Curiosity and facts: Griessmühle is known for its relaxed atmosphere and its focus on techno and electronic dance music. The club is also famous for its large outdoor area, which provides a great place to relax and enjoy the views over the city.

Advice: If you're planning to visit Griessmühle, be sure to dress comfortably, as the club has a relaxed dress code. It's also important to arrive early, as the club can get busy later in the night.

Getting there: Griessmühle is located in the Neuköllnneighborhood of Berlin, and can be easily reached by metro. The nearest metro station is Neukölln, which is just a short walk from the club.

Nearby attractions: Some nearby attractions include the East Side Gallery, the Berlin Wall Memorial, and the Simon-Dach-Straßeneighborhood.

COMPLETE LIST

ATTRACTIONS

SHOPS

MUSEUMS

THEATERS

GALLERIES

TOURS

WALKS